DEVELOPING
INTERCULTURAL
COMMUNICATION
SKILLS

The Professional Practices in Adult Education and Human Resource Development Series explores issues and concerns of practitioners who work in the broad range of settings in adult and continuing education and human resource development.

The books are intended to provide information and strategies on how to make practice more effective for professionals and those they serve. They are written from a practical viewpoint and provide a forum for instructors, administrators, policy makers, counselors, trainers, managers, program and organizational developers, instructional designers, and other related professionals.

Editorial correspondence should be sent to the Editor-in-Chief:

Michael W. Galbraith
c/o Krieger Publishing Company
P. O. Box 9542
Melbourne, FL 32902–9542

DEVELOPING INTERCULTURAL COMMUNICATION SKILLS

Virginia B. Ricard

KRIEGER PUBLISHING COMPANY
MALABAR, FLORIDA
1993

Original Edition 1993

Printed and Published by
KRIEGER PUBLISHING COMPANY
KRIEGER DRIVE
MALABAR, FLORIDA 32950

Library of Congress Cataloging-In-Publication Data

Ricard, Virginia B.
    Developing intercultural communication skills / Virginia B. Ricard.
        p.   cm. — (Professional practices in adult education and
    human resource development series)
        Includes bibliographical references and index.
        ISBN 0-89464-663-X (alk. paper)
        1. Intercultural communication.   I. Title.   II. Series.
    HM258.R47   1992
    303.48'2—dc20   92-11171
                                                                          CIP

10 9 8 7 6 5 4 3 2

CONTENTS

PART III.

THE SECOND PHASE OF THE FRAMEWORK:
YOUR SKILLS

PART IV.

THE THIRD PHASE OF THE FRAMEWORK:
ONGOING LEARNING

PREFACE

As part of an increasingly culturally diverse population in the United States, I have often felt we are challenged to be aware not only of our diversity but of the particular need to interact more effectively in our multicultural environments. The diversity present in this nation may be unequaled in any other country in the world. We have the opportunity here to learn to live together successfully—to work at it until we get it right—and to share our good results. I think we will.

In the meantime, there is much work to be done. The present era is marked by demographic changes, increased mobility of populations, and (not surprisingly) increased interaction among people within the United States with populations abroad. Interaction at home and abroad, though frequently successful, may only too often be difficult—discouraging or disappointing, at best, and violent, at worst.

What makes for success in intercultural communication? You will find some of the answers in this book and you will discover others through working with people. But success must be the focus of our efforts rather than concentrating excessive amounts of attention on what did not work in the past or what does not now result in positive outcomes. A consciously thought out plan, a framework for action, can be especially helpful in achieving constructive results as people from diverse cultures meet.

I view successful human interaction as a valuable goal of ongoing learning, an enriching ingredient of human development, and a stimulus for effective productivity. This philosophy is indeed reflected here in the nine chapters of this book which offer a framework for personal growth and the development of effective communication skills. I also recognize the need for appropriate resources—human and material—to help us when we need and want to know, to understand, to learn, and to change. You will note, therefore, the emphasis in this book on identifying, using, and evaluating these resources.

The three-part framework for growth presented in this book is focused on you (your needs, values, preferences, and roles), your intercultural communication skills, and your future skill development. The framework for growth introduced in Chapter 1 is followed in Chapter 2 by an overview of key factors that impact cultural relationships: attitudes toward commonality and diversity and toward the relationship of the individual to the group.

Chapters 3 through 8 are focused on key areas of intercultural communication skill development. These chapters highlight the key position of human values in interaction and enable you to apply theoretical concepts to areas of personal need. The six skill areas selected (valuing, observing, listening, thinking, speaking, and gesturing) are common elements across and between cultures and serve as an excellent basis for comparing and observing the influence of commonality-diversity and individual-group factors or values on human interaction.

Chapter 9 helps you look toward your future growth and development. The assumption is that your growth process will not end with the completion of this book but will be part of your learning for a lifetime.

Although the existing theoretical or research base is extensive regarding human interaction, the need for "how-to" or "theory-to-practice" approaches remains. More research is needed, especially across and between disciplines. We must be able to see ourselves as part of a dynamic and vital process, a person-focused, active process that impacts our own growth and that of others. Planned frameworks for personal action are clearly indicated, frameworks that encourage and allow us the flexibility of functioning effectively with others quite like us and with those who are not like us. There is room for many appropriate frameworks and I am offering one; this framework is built with my values—and maybe with some of yours.

This book is intended for persons working with or preparing to work with multicultural populations within the United States or abroad: adult educators; persons in human resource development and personnel or management areas; volunteers and specialists in the health professions, business or industry, and government.

Practicing professionals will find this book useful with adults both in classroom and training settings and in adult programs and community development projects as well. Practically speaking, the book will enable you to improve your intercultural communication in the following ways:

- Identify and develop intercultural communication and interaction skills in six key areas.
- Identify human responses to commonality and diversity.
- Recognize the influence of human values on the interaction process.
- Use a practical, flexible framework for ongoing learning and personal development in the area of intercultural communication and interaction.

I have presented a person-specific versus a culture- or country-specific focus and framework, not only because learning is person-centered and intercultural communication and interaction is an ongoing learning process, but because an abundance of resources related to diverse cultures and countries is available to you. For practice purposes, however, many examples in this book will pertain to the United States of America because we are here.

I feel the special need to present the information contained here in a practical way for direct transferal to your learning settings or worksites. I have, therefore, pooled the related research from the fields of anthropology, intercultural and international communication, education and training, and my own research and experience to address present-day needs. This resource will answer some of your questions regarding intercultural communication, but it should also help you see and develop important related skills in a new way.

ACKNOWLEDGMENTS

I wish to acknowledge the special contributions of those who made this book possible: my parents, Loraine and Raymond Hill, for their values and their example of sensitivity to human needs; my husband, Kenneth Ricard, for his ongoing encouragement of my intercultural interests and his unending support during the completion of this book; my friend, Alice Dowling, for demonstrating the value of intercultural communication and friendship; J. Roby Kidd and Malcolm S. Knowles, members of my Doctoral Committee, for sharing their knowledge of international adult education and self-directed learning for adults; John B. O'Hara, professor, for his insightful review of communication between cultures; Michael Galbraith, Mary Roberts, and Janet Kemerait, editors from Krieger Publishing Company, for their interest, suggestions, and special skills; and my friends from many cultures throughout the world who confirm and reaffirm the value of intercultural interaction.

THE AUTHOR

Virginia Ricard is an adult educator and consultant in the design and development of adult learning programs. She holds a B.S. in Chemistry from Marymount College of Kansas and, early in her career, worked as a Registered Medical Technologist (ASCP) in New York City. She lived abroad for seven years in Germany and in France and has traveled widely within and outside of the United States.

She has earned Masters of Education Degrees in Guidance and Counseling and in Adult and Continuing Education from Colorado State University and a Ph.D. in Adult Education from the Union Institute.

At Colorado State University, the University of Phoenix-Colorado Division, and at Regis University, she taught in undergraduate and graduate programs for adult learners. Her classroom presentations, workshops, and research have emphasized the application of theory to practice. The material she has developed for use by adult learners integrates related concepts across disciplines and supports self-directed learning techniques.

For the past 14 years she has concentrated on person-focused rather than country-specific approaches toward the improvement of intercultural communication and interaction. Her work has been oriented toward the identification of practical approaches which meet the needs of adult learners.

Part I

The Framework

CHAPTER 1

A Framework for Growth

The essential challenge of cultural diversity is that it highlights the need for more people to become involved in the business of understanding each other. Underlying this challenge is the realization that understanding, as part of the learning process, is person-centered and ongoing. Interaction is personal as well and cannot, therefore, be delegated (like driving) to others.

As part of a multicultural nation and world, we must not only recognize the importance of our individual roles in the development of human relationships but we must become actively engaged in the process of communicating and interacting effectively with others. In a world where it is possible for people from one hemisphere to be in another hemisphere within hours, or at most within several days, our own comfort level among people of other cultures may be directly related to our own actions and abilities.

Successful intercultural communication and interaction does not usually occur by chance. Rather, it is the result of exchanges and behavior on the part of persons who not only desire favorable results but have the skills necessary for generating and supporting positive outcomes. These skills may be yours—now or later—but, for success, a planned framework for their development appears essential.

WHY A FRAMEWORK?

For our purposes, planned frameworks are best described as consciously organized arrangements of related information that, because we are aware of them, influence our actions. In this book, our framework must not only arrange information to influence our actions but must enable us to balance (create a satisfactory climate for) interaction. For this reason, you might find it helpful to view the creation of this framework as a developing illustration or drawing in which major components of effective intercultural communications are clearly and flexibly outlined and the details are added by you to complete the picture. The details of your picture include information about your own knowledge, attitudes, and skills related to the area of intercultural communication and interaction.

Portions of your picture, or particular components of the framework, may be successfully developed more readily than others, depending on your personal strengths and learning needs. You will also need to become increasingly aware of any element of the framework, or of the picture you have already perhaps unconsciously created, that is the source of your present responses in the area of human interaction. That is, you will need to look closely at the mind set that you regularly use that guides your behavior during intercultural interaction. You may be less aware of the components of this picture, or mind set, if it has been developed over a period of years without conscious attention on your part. It is important, however, to recognize and evaluate all of the components of this picture. You may wish to retain and strengthen particular elements if you decide to make them a part of the newer, developing picture as other components are added. On the other hand, upon closer examination, you may find that some elements of your original mind set were inappropriate. Those elements should be eliminated from your framework.

Understanding the concepts introduced in this book will help you to focus your skill development on the knowledge and skills necessary for effective intercultural communication; you will learn to create a framework containing information and ongoing learning opportunities for constructive action. The use of the term framework in this resource, however, should not be confused with the concept of framing presented by Bateson (1972) or with descriptions by Goffman (1974).

A framework can be especially helpful to users in applying theoretical concepts to practice in everyday living situations. Four major reasons account for this observation:

1. Consciously organized frameworks provide a way of looking at a great deal of material and bringing it down to size for step by step practice. You may decide what elements to include or to exclude; what to emphasize or deemphasize; what to know and what to explore your feelings about; or what to do with the information.

2. Consciously organized frameworks provide a means of evaluating the progress you make when using a particular element of the framework and (importantly) provide a means of evaluating the relationship of parts of the framework to other parts and to the framework as a whole.

3. Elements of frameworks can be compared to elements of other frameworks.

4. Elements of frameworks can be changed or eliminated.

Decisions regarding the use of frameworks may lead to exciting or challenging discoveries and these decisions are yours. But, as mentioned earlier, deliberately designed frameworks are not the only frameworks to be highlighted for our purposes, and it is important to consider personal frameworks that may not be part of our awareness.

All of us view our worlds through culturally influenced frameworks that frequently collide with the different frameworks of others; this conflict makes us feel threatened. The degree to which we understand our own frameworks and the frameworks of others is often the degree to which we achieve unthreatened and successful human interaction. Nowhere is this achievement more observable than during interaction with multicultural populations, as in our own United States. Our personal frameworks are often determined by our cultures; to understand the significance of this observation, we must have an understanding of culture.

Culture

In the widest anthropological sense of the meaning of the term, culture is seen to include all of the accepted and patterned ways of behavior of a given people: their ways of thinking, feeling, and acting, and the physical manifestations of these. This broad definition enables us to view the values, beliefs, attitudes, and concepts of "self" of a given people as important to understanding their behavior. This view of culture allows us to recognize the influence of language and thought on activity and behavior; it allows us to recognize the importance of understanding conceptualizations regarding time and space, regarding race and ethnicity, or regarding religion, roles, status, and other factors.

For our purposes, therefore, the distinguishing characteristics of a people or culture might best be described as how the people think, feel, act, and appear. More specifically, *who* and *how* they are. Increased understanding of the beliefs, the attitudes, and the behaviors of people enables us to identify the similarities or differences that affect our ability to communicate effectively across cultures and to focus our efforts at skill development.

It is important to add here that the multi-dimensional aspects of this definition help a person or group **describe** their cultural heritage in terms of religious, racial-ethnic, language, or any other distinguishing factors. For example, this book is primarily designed for persons who would describe their national heritage as North American, of the United States (since Canadians are also Americans-North and Venezuelans are also Americans-South). Whatever other cultural factors make up our heritage, citizens of the United States share particular characteristics nationally. For many reasons, this book may be helpful to persons from other national cultures but the cultural "bias" (inevitably present) will reflect our own national values. The book also encourages users to utilize the tools presented in the following eight chapters to practice skill building within the United States among the multicultural populations here, as well as abroad.

Intercultural Communication and Interaction

Constructive interaction between culturally diverse groups is our ultimate goal. In this book, intercultural communication, the key to that constructive interaction, will refer to the ability of an individual or a group to achieve understanding through verbal and non-verbal exchange and interaction between cultures.

In order to achieve the goal of more effective intercultural communication, you must follow these three steps.

1. As you read in each chapter of this book the discussion of individual elements of communication, you must consider what preconceived ideas you have about this element and whether your own needs, values, preferences, and roles will make change in behaviors related to this element difficult.

2. Next you must determine what facts you already know about this element of the target culture, add new understanding through research, eliminate any misconceptions you may have held originally, and recognize your current skill development related to this element.

3. Then you must determine skills related to this element that would improve your communication with members of the new culture, and you must act to develop those skills, adding them to your framework for effective communication.

ESTABLISHING A FRAMEWORK

Because everyone establishes frameworks for action—consciously or unconsciously—frameworks are not the exclusive possessions of experts. They are sharable, consciously or unconsciously. In fact, the sharability of frameworks makes them a valuable exchange item in intercultural relationships because they allow others to see what you see and they enable you to see what others see to increase mutual understanding.

For example, frameworks for action may often be recognized in exchanges that begin with expressions such as "In our country we usually . . . " or "In our culture/family/religion we believe that . . . because . . . " or "I cannot eat . . . because. . . . " Although verbal exchanges may encourage direct sharing of frameworks, personal frameworks may also be discerned in non-verbal exchanges such as in the consistent avoidance of particular foods, in the exercise of particular religious practices, or in the exercise of customs regarding dress and adornment.

Sharing is possible, of course, when you recognize the frameworks, the influence of culture, and the components for your own actions. Benefits, too, are realized through the conscious sharing of frameworks and meaning, thus reducing the possibility of misinterpretation. Cultural attitudes toward sharing, however, may be as diverse as attitudes toward other cultural practices with some cultures valuing privacy over intercultural exchange.

WHY THIS FRAMEWORK?

Although the general uses of frameworks described above apply to the framework suggested in this book, the suggested framework in this text offers additional opportunities for growth. Because of the specific arrangement of its components, utilization of this framework will help you to:

- recognize yourself as actively engaged in improving intercultural communication and interaction;
- develop a self-directed, systematic process for skill development;
- identify your own values, attitudes, and learning needs; practice necessary skills and evaluate your progress;
- focus on two major relationship areas of human response that influence intercultural relationships and six areas for skill development.

All personal frameworks consist of components or parts from which action occurs at thinking, feeling, or doing levels. For example, the framework for growth presented in this book is focused on you, your skills, and your future skill development. The book is structured as a framework for these essential parts. To use the framework effectively, you will need to self-direct your learning, to practice the necessary skills, and to evaluate the results. The parts of the framework presented here are explained and illustrated.

However, all of the components of the frameworks for our diverse actions may not be understood by ourselves or by others. For example, it is possible for one of our actions to be observed but misunderstood by another—misunderstood, that is, from our own viewpoint since we have used our own framework to judge the action.

On the other hand, as mentioned earlier, we may not fully understand the makeup of one or more elements of our own frameworks, frameworks we use casually in daily encounters without questioning the basis for our actions or the accompanying thoughts and feelings.

Recognizing Parts

Recognition of the components of our own frameworks may be a necessary prerequisite to the successful development of additional frameworks and may represent a necessary area of concentration for you. The model in Figure 1.1 presents the major components of the framework for growth outlined in this book. In this suggested three-dimensional framework, your skill development is depicted as an active process initiated and controlled by you. The components of the first phase of development are basic to the focused skill development seen in the second phase and to the ongoing learning highlighted in the third phase.

The components of the first phase of development are focused on you and your knowledge of the relationship between commonality and diversity, your knowledge of the relationship between the individual and the group, and your ability to identify your own learning needs, values, preferences, and personal roles.

The second phase of development highlights six components that are common across cultures and that represent areas of skill building considered necessary for effective intercultural

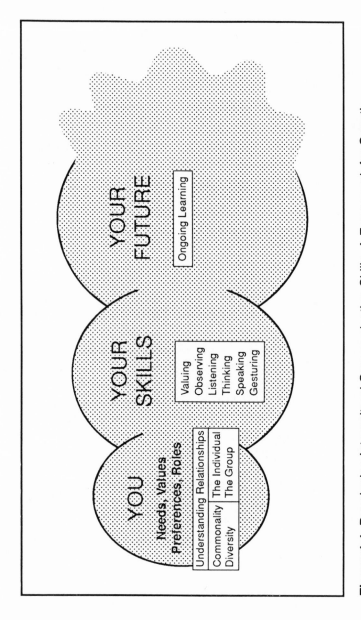

Figure 1.1 Developing Intercultural Communication Skills: A Framework for Growth

communication and interaction. These skill areas are valuing, observing, listening, thinking, speaking, and gesturing.

The third phase of development encourages and supports the process of ongoing future personal growth and skill development. This phase enables you to view the process of learning how to communicate and how to interact effectively with other people from other cultures as an area of active discovery for a lifetime.

The model presented in Figure 1.2 highlights three conceptual relationships or factors essential to understanding effective intercultural communication and to developing appropriate interaction skills. Components of the first phase of the framework, these key relationships are the relationships between

1. Commonality and Diversity

2. The Individual and The Group

3. Success- and Problem-Related Interaction

The influence of these relationships may be manifested in contrasting and various ways. For example, our understanding of the Commonality-Diversity factor could be demonstrated through our ability to distinguish between human similarities and differences within our own culture and within the cultures of others. An understanding of particular relationships between individuals and groups might be evidenced in our ability to identify the diverse cultural values or attitudes determining the independent, dependent, or interdependent functioning of individuals within a particular group. Our ability to distinguish between the characteristics of effective and ineffective communication within a particular culture would indicate a degree of understanding of the Success-Problem factor in human interaction. These factors and relationships will be addressed in Chapter 2.

The Influence of Attitudes

Although the recognition of the components of a framework is beneficial for personal growth and skill development, the

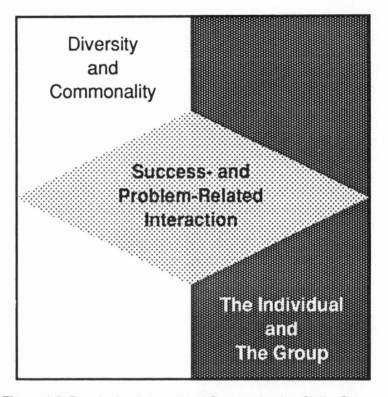

Figure 1.2 Developing Intercultural Communication Skills: Conceptual Relationship Factors

influence of attitudes must not be overlooked. Attitudes are related to or shaped by our personal values and directly affect what we decide to know, to understand, or to do, each of the three parts of the framework through which we view the world. As described in Chapter 2, attitudes will influence the direction and the level of your intercultural skill development.

SUMMARY

The framework for growth described in this chapter is a resource for ongoing personal intercultural communication skill development. The chapters to follow will present many different elements that together make up effective communication. Because different cultures have developed these elements in varied ways, you must consider each element first with respect to your own cultural behavior. Then you will need to determine the typical behavior for the new culture with which you interact. Finally, you might decide to modify your own behavior to avoid being misunderstood and to carefully observe the alternate behavior to avoid misunderstanding others. Attention should be directed toward the development of these skills through a close look at commonality and diversity and the relationship of individuals to groups, as discussed in Chapter 2.

Part II

The First Phase
of the Framework:
Understanding Yourself
and Your Relationships

CHAPTER 2

Understanding Relationships

This chapter is about you: your needs, values, preferences and roles. It is also about others—because that's what intercultural communication is about: you relate to others and others to you, with or without an awareness of the respective frameworks for action.

The basic components of understanding relationships, this first phase of the suggested framework for growth in intercultural communication, have been highlighted in this chapter, and attention has been given to the important factors that impact most intercultural relationships.

BALANCING RELATIONSHIPS

The use of the framework for growth suggested in this text may be seen as an attempt to establish "balance" in intercultural relationships, that is, to help us see our own frameworks in relation to the frameworks of others, to compare and contrast the components of both (in so far as possible), and to use or to develop the skills necessary for achieving effective communication. The idea (and the ideal), of course, is to be able to use the right skills in the right place at the right time and to support another person's efforts to do the same.

As suggested here, efforts to achieve balance in intercultural relationships are based on four key assumptions:

1. People of all cultures are worthy of respect.

2. People of all cultures can learn from each other.

3. Understanding improves intercultural relationships.

4. Behavioral adjustment in accordance with personal values may be helpful in intercultural interaction.

In practice, efforts to achieve balance may be especially difficult in the absence of appropriate skills or attitudes or if there is a lack of awareness regarding the frameworks we are presently using in interaction with persons of other cultures.

In balancing relationships, too, you will need to acquire an understanding of commonality and diversity, of how these factors are related and unrelated, and of how attitudes toward these factors influence successful interaction.

In Figure 2.1, balance in intercultural communication and interaction is shown as the result of skill development which has been based on a comparison of the components of your own framework and the components of the framework suggested in this book. You should begin this comparison as you complete this chapter and as you begin to identify in other chapters of the book any desired additional components for your own framework. As you begin this process of comparing the components of your own framework with components of the suggested framework, you will see that it is also possible for you to compare components from the frameworks of others with components of the suggested framework. These comparisons will become increasingly more useful as you seek to understand the people of a particular culture or to develop the skills that will be most helpful to you during interaction.

How does your present framework for action compare to the framework suggested in this book? Referring to Figure 2.1, you should begin now to prepare to answer this question. You can evaluate your progress by periodically repeating this question as you move through the three-dimensional suggested framework, the related activities, and the information included in each chapter of the book. For example, the major components of the first phase of the suggested framework contain information and activities focused on you, your skills, and your future. Highlighted components include your learning needs, values, prefer-

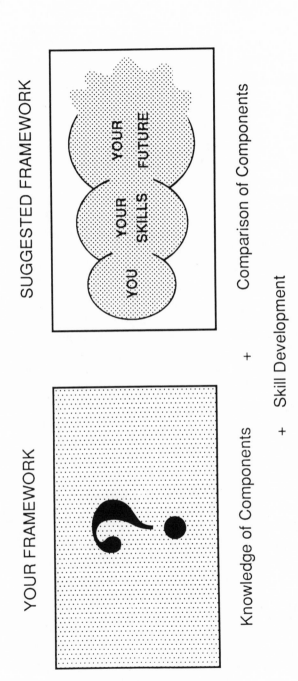

Figure 2.1 Framework Comparison

ences, and roles; your understanding of the relationship between commonality and diversity; and the relationship between the individual and the group. In the second phase skill related components include valuing, observing, listening, thinking, speaking, and gesturing. Ongoing learning related components complete the final phase of the framework.

It is important to see the three dimensions of the suggested framework as related rather than separated. Your learning needs, for example, are related to your focused skill development and to your future growth in intercultural communication. Your understanding of the relationship between the commonality and diversity and between the individual and the group is related to present and to future skill development.

Though you may not yet be ready to determine your learning needs based on a comparison of your listening abilities with those skills outlined in Chapter 5, you will be able to say whether or not these components are included in your own framework. Think about it. What are the components of your own framework for action at this time? Are you aware of the clusters of information on which your intercultural interaction is based? Are the skills you consider most important in intercultural communication related to the above-mentioned skill areas of valuing, observing, listening, thinking, speaking and gesturing? Which areas? Are your personal values part of your intercultural communication considerations? Does your framework include components that are not a part of the suggested framework? In your role at this time, which components in your framework do you consider most needed? Which of the suggested components might you consider adding?

As you complete the book, it will help you to think back to the framework comparison in Figure 2.1, to reevaluate your progress, and to determine any additional learning needs.

COMMONALITY: HOW ARE WE ALIKE?

Balancing a personal framework can be a challenging experience, however rewarding, particularly if you are unaware of some of the components of your own framework or if you suspect additions to that framework are necessary. Information and activities or practices are provided throughout this book that may become components of your own developing framework. You may gain insight, too, regarding some components in your framework that you may decide to discard as unrelated to your needs or to successful interaction. Whatever the case, however, an understanding of commonality is essential for effective intercultural skill development.

Needs and Characteristics

The common needs and characteristics of adults have been the focus of much research relevant to the practice of adult education and other disciplines. A popular example is the continued reference to and use of Abraham Maslow's Hierarchy of Human Needs (1954). With this model, Maslow illustrates the importance of satisfying human needs in ascending order within five significant areas: two basic areas related to the physiological or survival and safety needs of the individual; a higher level focused on the need for love and affection; another emphasizing the need for self-esteem; and a peak or highest level indicating the need for self-actualization or experiences related to the highest human potential. Maslow's model helps us better understand the actions of others (and of ourselves) that relate to one or more of the levels represented.

Malcolm S. Knowles (1970) has described six common adult needs or "motivating forces" that must be satisfied by every individual. In this concept, the forces are focused on the physical, personal growth, and security needs of the individual as well as on the desire for new experiences, affection, and recognition. Knowles suggests that the ways we satisfy these needs are influenced by factors common to us all: our needs are influenced by cultural forces in our surroundings and by our own interests, values, goals, or attitudes.

Although the factors just described are common conceptually and globally (that is, cultural forces surround all of us and we all have interests, values, goals, and attitudes), these factors appear diverse when translated into practice among individuals.

This view of a single factor in two contrasting configurations may be termed a "dual image." The dual image of a particular value such as wealth, for example, may be seen in the acquisition of property or money by members of a particular culture and in the giving away of property or money by members of another culture. The dual image of a particular attitude, such as the eating of meat, may be seen as embraced in one culture and rejected by another. The dual image of an idea, for example, may be seen simply as your image and my image. This "dual image" of particular factors must be recognized in comparisons of commonality and diversity and your ability to recognize dual images will be important in balancing relationships. The development of this skill enables you to view a familiar concept in a new way (even if you don't necessarily like what you see).

Particular characteristics are common to all people. For example, people in all cultures have the ability to communicate verbally and non-verbally, to speak and to hear. We transfer messages through signs and body movements or through touch, smell, and taste. The list of common characteristics is seemingly endless. People think, perceive, and interpret. All people express happiness and sadness; love and hate; anger and fear. All people grieve. People exhibit "personalities" and—throughout the world—hold certain values and attitudes. Knowledge, understanding, and preferences can be readily witnessed as people perform particular roles and demonstrate observable skills.

We even recognize common characteristics in certain activities. For example, we note the general tendency of adults to learn best when they feel the need for learning or the need to apply their learning.

These focused observations are especially important in developing an understanding of how we are alike. Excluding particular or obvious circumstances that may be readily explained and understood, the people of our world may be seen to have much in common. But what common factors are most important to us in determining a framework for action and improving our relationships, and are they really common?

The answers to these questions are not easy, and focusing on commonalities has always been difficult. One reason is that, inevitably, dual images will be encountered. For example, dual images may be present in a variety of circumstances varying from attitudes toward the presence or absence of hair on the head or body to values regarding the adequacy of housing and toilet facilities. Another reason focusing on commonalities has been difficult is that most of the research focused on "us" as a culture has been focused on "parts" of us or small groupings of people. Still another important reason is that most individual research is directed toward our own familiar areas and cultures—even within a particular culture and during periods of transition as in geographical relocations.

Ina Corinne Brown (1963, p. 154) emphasized the need to review "larger units" of a culture in order to understand the "modern world." Describing the rather global effect of cultural transition, she highlighted the "kind of revolutionary ferment that breaks down the barriers separating one kind of society and one kind of people from another" and viewed ideas as being "scattered to remote places as if they were seeds borne on the wind." Today, in a period marked by demographic changes and geographic relocations, a focus on the concept of commonality and its relationship to diversity appears even more necessary than before. We must not make the frequent mistake of assuming that what applies to some applies to all.

The commonality of communication described earlier has not only been explored by researchers but interpreted in a practical way by the noted anthropologist, Edward T. Hall. *The Silent Language* (Hall, 1959) provides an example of an important factor, with dual image, that must be recognized in understanding the concept of commonality:

> It must be remembered that when people talk they are using arbitrary vocal symbols to describe something that has happened or might have happened and there is no necessary connection between these symbolizations and what occurred. (p. 93)

In other words, all people speak or understand but speak or understand differently—for a variety of reasons. They are bound, in this case, by their own language systems.

If this is true, what factors should be considered in an effective framework for action? The answer to this question may be determined through consideration of those common factors that appear to have the greatest influence on our ability to relate effectively to each other.

Influencing Factors

Four obviously important factors common to all cultures might be considered: needs, values, preferences, and roles. Why? Because the needs of people directly affect the values they hold. The values (and related attitudes) influence their preferences, and individual preferences influence the roles they select and perform.

For our purposes, however, another and more complete response to the question of factors common to all people would require consideration of the following five key influencing factors: values and attitudes, knowledge and understanding, and observable skills. With this combination of factors, it is possible to see the relationship between the values people hold and the effect of those values on attitudes, the influence of attitudes on what is to be known and understood, and the resulting effect on skill development and interaction.

An additional advantage of this arrangement of factors should be noted. Cognitive, affective, and performance levels of human response are evident. These "feeling" (or emotional), "thinking" (or knowledge related), and "doing" (or demonstration) levels of action support a wide variety of learning options. And the balancing of relationships is best viewed as a learning experience to continue for a lifetime. Figure 2.2 illustrates the relationship between the five key influencing factors described above and the three levels of human response observed across cultures. Close observers of intercultural relationships will learn to recognize "feeling" level responses as related to the values or attitudes of a people, "thinking" level responses as knowledge-related, and "doing" level responses as related to observed skill areas.

The following definitions should be helpful in increasing

Influencing Factors	Levels of Response
Values and Attitudes	Affective "feeling" emotional
Knowledge and Understanding	Cognitive "thinking" knowledge
Observable Skills	Performance "doing" demonstration

Figure 2.2 Intercultural Relationships: Factors and Response Levels

your understanding of the factors outlined in Figure 2.2 and in balancing your frameworks.

- *Values*: beliefs, perceptions, and practices of worth to the individual
- *Attitudes*: preferences; decisions regarding personal roles and relationships to a group; orientation regarding the use of space and touch, discovery or learning, and human similarities and differences; self-esteem
- *Knowledge*: awareness or recognition of facts
- *Understanding*: perception; discernment; reasoning
- *Observable Skills*: ability to apply knowledge; learning and facilitating styles; verbal, non-verbal, and interaction modes; flexibility, dependency, independency, and interdependency patterns

Skill Areas

An understanding of the key factors that influence commonality in relationships would be incomplete without consideration of common skill areas, that is, those areas of communication skill development that particularly impact intercultural communication and interaction throughout the world. The six areas presented earlier in the framework for action include valuing, observing, listening, thinking, speaking, and gesturing. Although each area will be explored in succeeding chapters, the selection of these particular areas should be explained. (Caution! Dual Image Present!) All of these skill areas (or factors) are common to all cultures. The factors are person-focused and directly impact intercultural relationships. You control your own development and use of skills in each of these common areas.

DIVERSITY: HOW ARE WE DIFFERENT?

We may appear to be more different than we are the same and that seems to be a problem for us. Even when we are aware of our commonality and accept the essential realities of "sameness," we often experience difficulty dealing with differences.

Certainly our cultures are diverse, but however "common" a need or characteristic might appear in a particular area or culture, individual and small group differences must still be accomodated. An understanding of this diversity and its conceptual relationship to commonality can be especially helpful in building effective intercultural relationships.

Pluralism and Culture

In developing action frameworks, pluralism may be seen as a system embracing individuals or groups of diverse cultures. In pluralistic nations, such as the United States, this diversity is evident in the variety of socio-economic levels of our people, their physical and mental conditions, their racial-ethnic, religious, and educational backgrounds. Culture is viewed as all of the accepted and patterned ways of behavior of a given people, their ways of thinking, feeling, and acting.

With these definitions in mind, the challenges of intercultural relationships are apparent. Because the primary ingredient of culture is people, any understanding of the "seasonings" of culture should include (but not be limited to) family structure, values, racial and ethnic makeup, health, religion, communication and expression, sexual mores, food, and general social customs.

It probably isn't possible to know or to be able to do everything we would like to know or to be able to do to effect successful interaction. It is possible, however, to focus on the specific factors already identified as influencing intercultural relationships and to concentrate on learning related to these areas.

Influencing Factors

Values

Of all the factors presented in Figure 2.2, values must be considered the most important in any framework for action. Values are our connections to the things of worth to us in life. They are seen in our perceptions and beliefs and they are visible in our actions. As such, they are bound to our feelings and directly influence our attitudes. This influence can be observed in the variety of reactions to what is considered funny or shocking or to what is allowed or prohibited within a particular culture or between individuals.

Values vary across cultures and between individuals as evidenced in behavior. Consider, for example, the many contrasting ceremonies, practices, or patterns among cultures regarding life events such as birth, marriage, religious experiences, or death and burial.

Our values are nourished and protected and they guide our behavior. We speak of them being "held." Our values are valued.

Persons who develop the habit of searching for values find the process a rewarding journey into discovery. The search may begin with an informal self search or might be formalized through use of a values profile and related resources.

Using an informal self-search as a first step in developing effective intercultural communication, you should consciously evaluate your own values: which acts, customs, etc., do you regard in an especially favorable way? Which do you regard in an especially unfavorable way? Understanding of your own value bias will prepare you to react with understanding when you deal with a culture characterized by a value that is different from that espoused by your own culture.

Values vary among individuals because those values are so personal, and values vary across cultures because they are so social. That is, cultures and groups within the various cultures may have differing values and each attempts to ensure passage of these values to succeeding generations. Recognition of values related to a particular culture will not only enable you to interact with its members more effectively but this recognition will help you to expose to others your own, those cultural values important to you as an individual. Keep in mind the meaning of the term culture as defined for our purposes.

Attitudes

Too, if values are like the door to our human development, attitudes are like the hinges on which effective intercultural skill development depends during our growth. Attitudes directly influence preferences and individual decisions from choices of friends or clothing to the selection of careers and group affiliations. Our attitudes influence our reactions to odors or to food and they even influence how close to or how far from a person to position ourselves.

For example, studies regarding distance and the proxemic patterns of individuals and cultures indicate that these patterns vary across cultures and between individuals. Intimate, personal, social, and public distance has been described by Hall (1969), in a study within the United States, and by other researchers. Hall's findings illustrated areas of preference by comfort level and the involvement of individuals at close and far phase measurements in each category. The study reported cultural attitudes toward odors (skin and hair, lotion or perfume, body, foot and breath, or sexual odors) obviously implying their influence on distance preferences.

Attitudes toward race and ethnicity, skin color, or other physical characteristics may directly affect our openness to learning and to new experiences or to the development of friendships and understanding or self-esteem. In describing the lack of relatedness between race and behavior, Brown (1963) noted the influence of attitudes:

> Most of the criteria used by anthropologists in determining racial categories have to do with physical characteristics that are of little or no consequence in human behavior except as they are made so by the way people feel about them. (p. 11)

Attitudes are not inherited. They are acquired and they can be changed.

In supporting the value of cultural studies in our human development, Seymour Fersch (1974, p. 22) observed "The greatest value of cultural studies can be to help persons transcend their own cultural conditioning." Further clarifying the meaning, he adds, "By encountering contrasting minds—culturally different—each mind is reminded that its viewpoint is cultural rather than natural and its potential beliefs are not limited to its cultural inheritance."

The second step in achieving effective intercultural communication is to recognize the relationship between your personal values, determined above in step 1, and your attitudes. Following a self survey to recognize those attitudes, be aware that you will interact with people from other cultures, and that their attitudes will be different from yours because of their differing values. Be prepared to recognize these varied attitudes and determine whether you can treat them with tolerance and understanding in order to eliminate barriers to communication.

Knowledge

Our acquisition of knowledge, the third influencing factor in intercultural communication, may be affected by a variety of mental factors or conditions in addition to the influence of values and attitudes. Your willingness to identify and evaluate needed resources may be the key to maintaining a knowledge base for a lifetime. Who do you know who knows what you need to know? Who do you know who knows how to do what you need to be able to do? Where can you find the literary, audio-visual, or computer assisted resources that will help you? Formal or informal learning settings may be part of an answer, or visits with people who may not be like you in appearance, background, or behavior.

Understanding

Whatever the nature of your answers to these questions, movement from awareness to understanding, the fourth influencing factor, will require concentration and patience. For example, an awareness of the importance of learning or facilitating styles and an acceptance of individual differences in these areas may be a body of knowledge you wish to acquire. Accessing the resources and recognizing the key facts of interest to you, it will be necessary for you to relate these facts to the special needs you might have on the job, or during travel and interaction opportunities.

Knowledge is personal and pleasurable. You know!

Understanding is social and satisfying. You appreciate!

Knowledge and understanding are essential factors in building interpersonal relationships.

Skills

Of the factors in Figure 2.2 which influence intercultural relations, observable skills, the fifth factor, are the ones most likely to be recognized by other people. The other factors may or may not "show" so readily in public but the skills factor does "hang out." Our behavior is on display and it is truly a time for competency. Because the roots of competency are embedded in knowledge and practice, the determination of learning needs should be given priority consideration.

An awareness of your own observable skills learning needs

can be especially helpful in developing the skills necessary for your framework for action. The process need not be complicated. A simple self-evaluation will suffice if your questions to yourself are targeted toward the most pressing needs and your responses are complete. Question yourself about how you learn best and about your personal needs, values, preferences, and roles. Ask questions: "What have I learned within the past three years that was especially helpful to me? How and where did I learn it? Why?" "What do I do especially well (and not so well) when I am communicating with people from other cultures?" "What would I like to be able to do that I have not yet done or that I am unable to do when communicating with people from other cultures?" "How do I feel about the people of this particular culture?" "What do I know about the people of this culture?" "What shall I do about the learning needs I have identified?"

Your self evaluation will not only be useful in directing your own skill development but will alert you to the development of others in these areas and will direct your behavior accordingly. For example, if you enjoyed a recent learning experience as a participant in a workshop setting because you were able to "learn by doing," you might look for a similar practical experience related to intercultural communication. If you communicate well verbally in another language but your role demands written communication in the language, you may need to address the development of that skill. If you express negative feelings about the people of a particular culture, and if you do not know much about them, you may decide to learn more through reading, through discussing with knowledgeable, experienced persons within and outside of the culture, through using audio-visual materials, or through finding other approaches, particularly those that suit your own learning style.

THE INDIVIDUAL-GROUP RELATIONSHIP

A chapter on understanding relationships would not be complete without highlighting another key area of understanding that is necessary for developing an effective framework for action and intercultural relationships. Groups are composed of individuals and individuals bring diverse needs, values, preferences, and roles to any particular group. The group *is* affected by the presence of the individual and the individual *is* affected by the presence of the group—whether or not these influences are recognized and acknowledged.

Our initiation as members of a group begins with birth and that "group" extends to include the world. Think of it. We become part of a family which is part of a community of families which is part of a nation of families which is part of a world of families.

From another perspective, we live in a geographical area which is part of a larger geographical area which is part of a still larger geographical area of the world. And our world becomes smaller as technology links us with increasing speed.

Although our individual group affiliations begin with the family, extended affiliations may include groups at local, national, and international levels. It is important for us to recognize these relationships in order to realize our own positions in the world.

At world level, the needs, values, preferences, and roles of individuals are usually recognized and acknowledged as diverse. Would anyone describe us as all the same—really? The problem is that our collective responses to needs may be fragmented or tangential or frequently nonexistent. For example, response to the needs of women has been described as generally inadequate throughout the world. In this example, gender considerations are skewed.

In other instances, diverse individual needs may pass unrecognized by groups or may remain submerged as these groups move toward the achievement of their primary goals to satisfy the general needs: The group comes first! There are other examples of group goals and needs remaining suspended as individuals satisfy their own needs: The individual comes first!

A certain tension exists between the satisfaction of individual needs and the satisfaction of group needs. This tension is present in small and large groups or cultures. Recognition of this dynamic within a given culture or group is necessary for balancing relationships in multicultural settings.

SUCCESSES AND PROBLEMS IN INTERACTION

Successful intercultural communication and interaction patterns are not always easily achieved but the marks of successful interaction are readily observable. These marks should be noted carefully as you work toward greater skill development. The characteristics of problem interaction must be recognized, as well, with emphasis on preventive approaches during skill development.

Success

In successful interaction, people are actively involved. Although they bring different values, attitudes, knowledge, understanding, and skills to the setting, the participants are participating.

In successful interaction, people evidence interest and their attitudes are positive regarding the activities. Their enthusiasm is visible and they feel comfortable being together. The participants share common interests.

In successful interaction, people demonstrate an openness to discovery. They learn. Participants "risk" exposure to new experiences and view these experiences as "new beginnings." How these marks of success are evidenced may obviously vary from individual to individual and from culture to culture. They are, however, observable across cultures.

Problems

Problems in intercultural communication and interaction are also visible to interested observers.

Problem interaction may be present when the participants are uncomfortable with commonality or diversity. They resist acknowledging the existence of similarities or differences between people. They have difficulty interacting with people who are not like themselves or, conversely, they confine interaction to persons unlike themselves.

Problem interaction may be present when participants have difficulty accepting their own roles within the group. They resist recognizing or acknowledging group norms and values. They view their identity as diminished when part of a "whole" or group.

Problem interaction may be present when participants lack the knowledge or skills necessary for successful interaction. They do not know what to do or are unable to do what needs to be done. They do not want to know or to do what needs to be done and they avoid practicing.

SUMMARY

Performance in intercultural settings can be improved through an understanding of the relationship between commonality and diversity and the important individual-group dynamic. Skill building should be focused on personal growth needs and related to the six factors that directly influence the interaction process. Specific skill areas include valuing, observing, listening, thinking, speaking, and gesturing. Valuing will be addressed in Chapter 3.

Part III

The Second Phase of the Framework: Your Skills

CHAPTER 3

Valuing

As the first of six chapters focused specifically on intercultural skill development, "Valuing" expands the information on values that you have already covered in earlier chapters to include the impact of values on skill development. Important areas of consideration include family, religion, health, status relationships, and the use of time.

THE ROLE OF VALUES

For our purposes, values have been defined as beliefs, perceptions, and practices of worth to the individual. Values have also been described earlier as the "door" to our human development because they are visible across cultures among all of the world's people and they relate to almost every area of our daily living. Values are reflected in personal preference and influence the attitudes that develop. They are, therefore, diverse, although frequently shared by members of a particular culture or group.

Personal Values

One way to begin to understand the role of values is to look at your own values. The 24 values listed in Figure 3.1 have been selected from the 154 values in the "Look" Values Profile in *ACCORD* (Ricard, 1979) and illustrate the diverse nature of adult values that influence intercultural interaction.

How would you rate these values in terms of their impor-

I value . . .
1. Clean air
2. Seclusion
3. Dependability
4. Convenience
5. Smoking
6. Belief in God
7. Family
8. Promptness
9. Cooperation
10. Group responsibility
11. Intelligence
12. Interaction with members of my own culture(s)
13. Informality in relationships
14. Character
15. Diffusion of power/authority
16. Problem-solving
17. Verbal expression
18. Knowledge
19. Interaction with members of other cultures
20. Independence
21. Competition
22. Art
23. Physical space
24. Religion

Figure 3.1 Twenty-four Selected Values

tance to you? Take a few moments to review the list, indicating the level of importance as Zero (0), Low (L), Moderate (M), or High (H). Which five values are *most* important to you? Which five values are *least* important to you?

This brief look at your own personal values may help you to understand your own behavior. If you are working with multicultural groups, it might be helpful to know the importance of these values (and others) to them. Facilitators in a learning setting, for example, might be interested in knowing the general preferences within a group for informality in relationships, for problem-solving activities, or for personal independence so that methods and approaches could be adjusted accordingly. Too, persons from the United States who are working abroad might be better able to understand the preferences of others in the workplace regarding verbal expression, competition, or physical space.

Group Values

Although the responses of individuals may vary, it is possible to observe similarities in the larger group response as a whole. That is, the preference for a particular value may be the same for a number of group members. The ratings of individuals using the profile across the United States might vary but similarities in group response could be noted. In the same way, individual ratings throughout the world might vary, but similarities could be noted among the responses. These similarities in responses enable us to see the preferences and values of larger and of smaller groups or cultures.

It is important to note that a group *is* a "culture." The individual members bring an assortment of values to the group that reflect similarities and differences but it is the similarities that usually surface in their goals and actions or practices. Values are reflected in what people do, not only as individuals, but in groups as a whole.

All of the values presented in Figure 3.1 may influence the responses of persons during intercultural interaction and all of the values relate to personal preferences and attitudes. Of the 154 values in the "Look" Values Profile, certain values may evoke similar responses across the United States and may influence the behavior of North Americans from the United States at home and abroad. The purpose of this book is not to present a country-specific but a person-focused framework for intercultural interaction. It is important, however, to realize that we function from a country-specific as well as a person-specific framework, whatever our cultural heritage, and that we exhibit this duality in our behavior. This duality is reflected in the values we hold and identify or include in a personal values profile. We bring the only values we have to any setting and recognize them among the values of others. Interaction problems generally arise, however, when we expect that our values are shared by others and they are not. For this reason, particular values that are familiar to persons of a United States-based North American culture should be recognized as important in our behavior.

Values Common to the Culture of the United States

Edward C. Stewart (1975) has described the assumptions, values, and behavior of Americans and what he views as numerous contradictions between these factors. Stewart notes the tendency of persons to view their assumptions as "reality" and to be surprised when these assumptions are not interpreted by others as "reality" because they have another set of assumptions. Members of a particular culture may not be aware of the assumptions influencing their behavior and when confronted with inferences, or when questioned, may refuse to acknowledge the assumptions even to themselves.

A detailed look at values in this country has been offered by Stewart whose work has been focused on topics that are bound to attract the attention of anyone already interested in effective intercultural interaction. The topics are as follows: perceptions of self, the self as a point of reference, systems of thought, self-reliance, the belief that man is separate from nature, materialism and property, achievement and progress, characteristics of personal relations, equality, confrontation, fragmentation and totality of the personality, informality and formality, friendship, personalization and depersonalization, cooperation and fair play, the need to be liked, role specializations, comparative judgments, and form of activity abroad. Consider your own cultural values in each of the above areas and then research the same topics for your target culture as you work to develop skills that enable you to recognize the cultural values of others.

It is not possible or desirable to address here a large number of values that influence our behavior during intercultural interaction but particular influencing values (Ricard, 1991) should be mentioned. These values (listed below) may influence interaction positively or negatively—depending on the values of others around us—and include the following:

- *Independence*: A prominent, visible value that influences our behavior in the United States; it is reflected in our general preference for individual and group pursuits that emphasize the freedom to achieve in directions of our own (and the group's) choice
- *Action/results*: A value commonly observed in our general need to "do something" and to "get it done", to realize concrete outcomes
- *Verbal Interaction*: A value generally and actively present and preferred in our communication within the United States
- *Happiness*: A readily observed value expressed in our general need to "feel good" about situations or things and to have others feel the same
- *Quickness*: A value evident in our general efforts to "get it done as soon as possible" and not to "waste time"
- *Courtesy*: A value expressed in our general need to acknowledge the presence, kindness, or services of others, to evidence respect
- *Equality*: A value present in our generally expressed opinion that "everyone is created equal" and our general efforts to see that "everyone has a chance"

When the values of others around us are similar to those described above, the interaction may be successful. When the values of others are dissimilar, or our behavior is misinterpreted, the interaction may be difficult.

Our behavior may precipitate difficult interaction, for example, if we are encouraging individual approaches within a group and group members value cooperative methods or direction from a designated authority. Interaction may become difficult if we design highly paced programs for use with persons who value slow or moderately paced interaction or if we emphasize "getting right to the point" when discussion and extended interaction is valued.

Dependence on the verbal aspects of communication may be thwarted or blocked (with resulting frustration) in interaction where others value the use of non-verbal forms of communication.

Courtesy may be valued in all cultures but the manner in which courtesy is extended may vary greatly between individuals and between cultures or groups. Values influence customs and customs usually determine the forms courtesy will take. Interaction may be difficult if we are unaware of the common and expected courtesies valued by members of a particular group.

Interaction may be difficult when we don't "feel good" about titles or positions or ranks and those around us value them, or when we "want to offer a chance" to others and they believe conditions are acts of fate.

Courtesy and independence, happiness and quickness, action and results and equality are important to us but concern for the values of others can be present as well, and successful interaction can be achieved without threat to our own value systems if we work at developing the necessary skills.

THE IMPACT OF VALUES ON SKILL AREAS

Because values are related to so many aspects of our daily life, those areas where the impact of values is greatest should receive attention, for example those areas related to attitudes, knowledge, and performance.

Attitudes

The influence of attitudes on personal growth was addressed in Chapter 2 but we will focus on understanding particular relationships among people in this chapter.

Individual-Group Relationships

One important relationship is that of the individual to the group; this relationship was also addressed in Chapter 2 and it is a relationship that must be recognized in intercultural interaction. Acting upon our cultural preferences for independent action and results-oriented movement within groups that value joint, open ended discussion-oriented movement may end in disappointment for everyone. Thus the relationship of the individual to the group may be manifested in diverse ways that are observable. In cultures which value responsibility to the group first and to the individual as part of that group next, decisions and movement may be reflected in the provision of facilities, sites, activities, or resources for the common good and efforts to insure equalized distribution with centralized control. In cultures that value responsibility to the individual first and to the group next, decisions and movement may be directed toward individualized satisfaction of needs and toward efforts to provide limited common resources with distribution of these resources through decentralized control. In some cultures, a single person or a few individuals decide for all; in other groups, all members make the decisions that affect individual behavior.

Whatever the case, the relationship of the individual to the group is a key factor in interaction, and knowledge of this dynamic must be a part of any personal cultural action plan. In practice, you will need to be able to recognize the values and attitudes present in individual-group cultural behavior, your own values, and those of others; you will need to be able to direct your personal response and to evaluate this learning experience.

Adult-Youth Relationships

Another important area of observation is the cultural attitude of individuals and groups toward adult-youth relationships. These attitudes, too, vary both across cultures and between individuals. Values within a particular culture may be observed in families; in adoption and parenthood patterns; in the organizations, activities, and services available to youth; in opportunities for youth involvement; in roles and degrees of youth involvement or participation; in types of recognition; and in child abuse ratings.

Brown (1963, p. 37) has reported practices in which a husband, wife, and children shared a household but the mother's brother was responsible for disciplining the child and establishing a place for the child in the community, and it was from this brother that the child received an inheritance of "wealth, magical knowledge, status and rank."

In some societies, when a woman is widowed, her husband's family will be responsible for her and her children. In other societies, the paternal grandmother makes the major decisions regarding a child. The assignment of special roles supports the need for security and belonging.

In patrilineal clans, descent traced through males, the children belong to the clan of their father; in matrilineal clans, they belong to the clan of their mother. Clan members are usually expected to help each other and often assume responsibility for children other than their own.

Brown (1963, p. 42) has also described the importance of understanding the way some cultures group their relatives (according to generation) and the ways others classify relatives considering factors we may ignore or misunderstand. For example, in our classifications we in the United States do not consider age, or relation to us by birth or marriage, or whether relatives are on the mother's or the father's side. The classification patterns of many cultures, in relating through the father or through the mother, may consider the father and his brothers "father" to the child and the wives of these "fathers" as "mothers" to the child. In other societies, there are no words which can be translated simply as brother or sister, niece or nephew because the sex of the **speaker** is considered rather than the person in question. Knowledge of kinship patterns such as these and others is helpful because it reflects the attitudes (and the values) of people toward adult-youth relationships. Kinship networks serve to support group and individual needs from childbirth through the rearing period into adulthood, a necessary function—though patterned unlike our own support systems.

Your approach to skill development in this area should again include the identification of the values represented in intercultural interaction, consideration of your own response, and evaluation of the learning experience.

Male-Female Relationships

General attitudes toward male-female relationships represent another important learning area for understanding relationships. Values related to these attitudes may be reflected in families; in organizations, activities and services available to women; in marriage and parenting patterns; in opportunities for female involvement; in roles and degrees of involvement and participation; in types of recognition; and in female abuse ratings.

Values may be passed to succeeding generations through family traditions, customs, and practices, and wide variations are observed among cultures. Most cultures "assign" roles to family members according to gender and these roles may be carried out, with few alterations in "job descriptions," over extended periods of time and with little or no relationship to changes occuring in the external or social environment. Within some cultures, roles may be assigned according to gender with little or no consideration of personal needs, interests, or capabilities. Role assignment may be more flexible in particular cultures than others but, in general, men rather than women have determined the direction of economic, civil, and religious movement and have occupied the majority of positions of authority. Even in matrilineal societies familial authority is usually vested in a particular male, and in many cultures women do most of the work.

Public demonstrations of affection between men and women may be a concern in many cultures and practices vary, some groups prohibiting these practices, others tolerating the actions, and still others ignoring the displays. The subject may be an important consideration for Americans abroad because they generally value informality and friendliness and affection may be openly expressed in many parts of the United States, frequently accompanied by hugging or kissing. Brown (1963, p. 102) has described the reaction: "To many peoples, the Western practice of kissing, especially in public is regarded as shocking behavior."

Understanding These Relationships

Your own understanding of the relationships described above will be increased if your approach to skill development in each area (individual-group, adult-youth, and male-female relationships) includes a review of your own knowledge of each area. What do you know about the people involved and their localities? What do you know about your own values and intercultural communication skills? How similar or different are your cultures?

The needs assessment presented in Figure 3.2 will help you identify your knowledge-related strength and need areas. For each item in each section, indicate your level of knowledge as Absent (0), Low (L), Moderate (M), or High (H).

A comparison of your ratings from Figure 3.1 (values) and Figure 3.2 will help you identify particular areas for skill development. Select one or more areas for practice and begin to identify appropriate resources (literary, audio-visual, human) to assist your development. Practice may not make perfect but you will improve your ability to function effectively in intercultural settings.

Knowledge

Deciding what to learn is a personal activity that is best guided by you toward the areas that please you most. For this reason, you were encouraged to recognize your attitudes, to search for your values, to determine your responses, and to evaluate your own progress. Knowing that you **want** to know often leads to knowing what you **need** to know to function effectively.

You are encouraged to observe, to question, and to determine what you think might be happening in a particular cultural situation and to notice how the action is developing. For example, attending a religious ceremony that is unfamiliar to you, you

1. What do I know about the *people*?
   Language
   Racial-ethnic composition
   Religion
   Values
   Social customs
   Food preferences
   Health
   Non-verbal expressions
   Education
   History
2. What do I know about the *area*?
   Geography
   Private sites
   Public facilities
   Private facilities
   Socio-economic factors
   Business
   Social support systems
   Government
3. What do I know about *my* . . .
   Values?   Role?
   Intercultural communication skills?
4. What do I know about the similarities and the differences between *our* cultures?

Figure 3.2 Needs Assessment

might begin to understand the significance of the experience by closely observing the setting for the event, the activities, the sequencing of the activities, and the persons involved; you might then attempt to discover the aim of the action or the obvious result of the action.

You now need to ask *why* things are happening. The answer to this question will help you understand the values and customs represented in intercultural interaction. Using the above example, the ceremony might be a sacrificial offering or a celebration of marriage, birth, or death; a membership initiation, a spiritual cleansing, or a renewal ritual. These practices are usually related to the spiritual, religious, or social beliefs of a given people and reveal their cultural values.

A process suggested in *ACCORD* (Ricard, 1979) may help you identify knowledge areas of interest to you. The values you identify—your own and those of others around you during intercultural interaction—not only relate to particular needs, preferences, knowledge and roles, but might be categorized as those values related to an area, its people, and your position in the area. This information may be useful at home in the United States or abroad.

For example, your own value-based concerns and the value-based concerns of others might relate to the environment and may be focused on land use, climate, or pollution. Other concerns may be people-focused and include considerations related to jobs and careers, dress or racial-ethnic factors. Concerns related to your own position might include concerns about your duties, or about the frequency of interaction with peers, other Americans, and the local populations.

Assessing Personal Needs

Here, too, a self-assessment might be helpful in determining your personal learning needs. This assessment works best if kept simple. Ask the question "What do I know about. . . . ?" and determine your level of knowledge on a four-point scale, ranging from no knowledge through low or moderate to a high level.

For example, "What do I know about **farming** in this area?" (Level: low). "What do I know about the **social dress codes** of these people?" (Level: high). "What do I know about use of the **local language** and **my job**?" (Level: high).

Customs of a local population within or outside of the United States will provide enough knowledge challenges! These challenges may be found as you enter another "culture" when you move from the inner city to a small farming community, from north to south or east or west, and from the United States to another country. What you know or need to know about the area, its people, and your position there must be determined.

Recognition of values is the first step toward building a knowledge base, but recognition of your own learning need areas must follow if you are to practice building skills, and skill building is a personal task. Your role (and challenge) will be to identify these knowledge areas of need but also to include information related to formality and informality patterns, race and ethnicity concerns, and local customs.

Formality and Informality

Questions regarding our own values may arise when attitudes toward particular behaviors are contrasted. Informality in relationships is so commonly accepted within the United States that it may not be questioned in many parts of the country or between individuals. In other parts of the country, informal behavior may not be readily accepted or, in some instances, may not even be tolerated.

Informality can be recognized in our private and public behavior, our patterns of dress, and our social courtesies. Informality "shows" when we are addressed by our first name at a drive-in bank, wear shorts to church, or encourage a new acquaintance to "drop over anytime." One or more of these practices may be unacceptable when interacting with other cultures.

On the other hand, persons who are comfortable with informal behavior may be uncomfortable with formal behavior or in formal settings within or outside of the United States. Problem interaction may occur when we are unaware of, or unable to accept, the need for doing something to balance the interaction. Recognizing the values present helps us balance actions, and having the necessary knowledge and skills helps us balance intercultural interaction. One way of looking at the balancing process is to realize that attitudes help us decide to do something; having the knowledge helps us know what to do; and having the skills helps us do whatever we decide to do.

For example, on discerning the discomfort of others with informal behavior, we might altar our own to match the existing local norms, but we must be aware of the local norms (knowledge) and practice (skill area) the necessary skills in order to achieve successful interaction.

Altering Behavior

Alteration of behavior may not be difficult when a "clash" of values is not presented during interaction, but may be an area of concern when a particular value is highly important to you and of little or no importance to others around you. And what happens when the behavior expected of you is unacceptable to you?

You will need to respond, of course, and you will have to determine the nature of your response. These cultural value dilemmas may be difficult but recognition of the values and development of a knowledge base can be especially helpful. Often you will have an opportunity to prepare for interaction in advance; if you have time to prepare for a particular experience, it pays to know as much as possible about an area, its people, and your position within the area. You will need to know as much as possible about your own values if you have little or no time to prepare for an experience.

Racial-Ethnic Factors

Knowledge of racial-ethnic factors is particularly important in the development of personal skills. In many cultures, attitudes toward racial and ethnic differences are a major cause of value clashes. In cultures where persons are primarily related to the same racial group, few social difficulties may be encountered within the culture, but conflict may surface when encountering differences outside the culture. In pluralistic groups or cultures

with people of many racial-ethnic backgrounds, conflicts may
occur with varying frequency and duration or intensity, depending on the composition of the group or culture and the nature
of the conflict. The racial-ethnic groups represented may or may
not interact on a regular basis or may interact with varying degrees of selectivity, perhaps choosing to interact with one or
more groups and to avoid interaction with others.

John Leo (1991) described the variation in feelings in an
article titled " 'Diversity' tears oneness in two":

> For five years, Washington debated whether the Smithsonian's
> major new project on black heritage would be a 'free-standing'
> building or a 'major wing' of the National Museum of American
> History.
>
> The emphasis on black culture is welcome and overdue, but the
> separatist symbolism is appalling. It means that fewer whites will
> be exposed to black exhibits, and fewer blacks to those of the
> main museum. (p. 28)

The degree to which members of various racial-ethnic
groups or cultures interact determines the degree to which they
recognize the values of the others. Values must be exchanged and
experienced to be known because they are present in the ideas
and practices of all people. The dimensions of acculturation
stress and coping have been described by Dyal and Dyal (1981)
in a study of immigrant populations. In general, observable differences are the focus of most difficult intercultural interaction
because they appear to be "the problem" when the "problem"
is more frequently related to attitudes, and the attitudes are related to values. People may, for example, spend a great deal of
time looking for things in others that are just like their own.
These similarities may vary from skin or hair coloring and racial
background to language and music or art related interests. Many
may live, work, play, worship, and learn with people who are
very like themselves. Others interact daily with persons from a
variety of backgrounds and with interests quite unlike their own.
An article by Chaze (1980) in U.S. News and World Report described the historic bias that often awaits newcomers such as the

refugees who have come to the United States from all over the world since World War II. Discriminatory practices related to hiring or which limited access to economic advancement opportunities and housing often complicated the process of resettlement. The process was often more stressful for some groups than for others, particularly for people of color, and often for persons fleeing from areas that had been engaged in fighting with forces from the United States. Racial-ethnic slurs and misunderstanding of cultural customs or practices on the part of some persons in the receiving communities often made daily life more difficult for the newcomers.

Dealing with difference may be threatening to us because it involves the possibility of change; change is resisted until realized (that is, a new condition, structure, or organization replaces the old) and the resistance pattern is again resumed. For example, it is sometimes risky to try a new food because if we try it, we might like it. That would mean adding an item to a "menu" that was already familiar to us and that we really thought was fine anyway and "buying" the necessary ingredients might be an additional cost. The unknown can be threatening.

Racial-ethnic differences not only represent an area of the unknown to many but attitudes toward the known and recognized differences have often been influenced by cultural myths. When people don't know and don't understand each other, they often create images of their own which are shared with others to become stereotypes. Stereotypes often develop because an observed characteristic has been tailored to fit the needs or purposes of an individual or group. If, for example, a person believes that the color of his or her skin is preferable to that of others and wants other people to agree, that person may propose a negative image of other skin colors to sell the concept and to preserve the preference. Preservation of the preference is necessary for, if the preference is recognized as based on false assumptions, the person might be viewed as having made a poor choice. Because the choice must be supported, the negative image may be seen to grow larger and larger. The known (skin color) has become an unknown (negative image) that is viewed as "known" on the basis of attitudes.

In a study of the difficulties encountered in communicating interculturally, Samovar and Porter (1976) noted the following:

> Attitudes are psychological states that predispose us to act in certain ways when we encounter various social events or objects in our environment. Not only do attitudes influence our overt behaviors, they also cause us to distort our perceptions—that is, to interpret events so they are in accord with our predispositions. (p. 9)

Prejudice or pre-judgment of people or things or situations is the conduit for stereotypes, and prejudice affects intercultural interaction because it blocks the road to discovery and learning.

The decision to explore the unknown may be risky but challenging, and it can be exciting and growth producing. Many unknowns are present in intercultural interaction but the prospect of interacting successfully may be worth the effort to us. The perceived risks encountered through interaction, whether based on differing customs or practices or language, may be channels to discovery; and the outcomes of discovery—learning—represent growth.

Performance

The key to effective performance in intercultural interaction is the ability to match your learning needs to areas of knowledge that will improve your understanding and then to develop related skills and to practice using these skills. It will help you if you see your learning needs as related to feeling, thinking, and doing levels. These levels are related to your values and attitudes, knowledge and understanding, and (importantly) performance.

Feeling, Thinking, and Doing Levels

In determining your needs at feeling level, keep in mind that these are the needs that relate to your values and attitudes. You will discover them by answering the questions "How do I feel about . . . ?" or "What do I believe about . . . ?" or "What is my attitude toward . . . ?"

To discover thinking needs that relate to your knowledge and understanding, answer the questions *"what* do I know about . . . ?" or *"how* does . . . happen (or work or function)?" and *"why* is . . . true (or that way or happening)?" *"why* do I believe (or value or think or feel) this?"

Knowing is having the information or being aware of the information you need in order to perform; understanding is being able to relate the information you have in order to perform. The ultimate goal of study is to develop appropriate skills and to use them.

Matching Needs and Activities

Matching the needs you have identified to performance means selecting activities of your choice at feeling, thinking, or doing levels. For example, if you are considering feeling-level needs, select activities that enable you to explore the need at feeling level. You might complete a values profile or an attitude survey or identify your feelings about practices which reveal the values of others. To identify activities for a need at thinking level, you might participate in a discussion or seminar related to the group or culture of interest or read material related to the need or use video tapes and films related to the need.

To identify activities for needs at performance level, develop and present information related to the need; design and develop materials that meet the need, or participate in a related intercultural experience.

The aim of the process above is to use

- feeling activities to meet feeling needs;
- thinking activities to meet thinking needs; and
- doing activities to meet doing needs.

The activities in Figure 3.3 from *ACCORD* (Ricard, 1979) provide examples of activities at feeling, thinking, and doing levels which you will recognize. Your values, too, may be recognized

1. Avoid displaying a favorite valuable possession.
2. Avoid using an electric or gas (a) washer, (b) dryer, or (c) stove.
3. Look for symbols related to the new culture which are similar to and different from symbols in your own culture.
4. Use the metric system of measurement.
5. Except for the essential items, remove most of the furniture from one room.
6. Sit or stand closely (within one foot) to at least two persons you do not know.
7. Lower your eyes when speaking to a person of the opposite sex.
8. Look for similarities and differences between the United States and the new culture related to (a) rights, (b) odors, (c) tastes, (d) sounds, (e) feelings, (f) beliefs, and (g) behavior.
9. Make a distinction between your own opinion and U.S. Government policy when responding to related questions about the United States.
10. Respond knowledgeably and adequately to questions regarding the United States by persons presently in this country but from other cultures.

Figure 3.3 Intercultural Relations and Skill Building Activities

in these activities. If some of the activities are related to learning needs that you have already identified, you might wish to practice the related skills and to evaluate your progress.

You will need to decide

- if or how an activity relates to the area you are visiting;
- if or how the activity is to be used to meet your particular learning need;
- how much time you will allow for the activity;
- when and how often you will repeat the activity; and
- whether you will practice the activity at home or abroad.

THE IMPACT OF VALUES ON PREFERENCES

The values present in our preferences essentially influence almost every area of our daily lives, for example our preferences for particular foods, cosmetics, pets, religions, friends, or medicines. The impact of preferences on our lives is great but discussion must be narrowed, for our purposes, to focus on five areas that are important within our culture. An understanding of these areas may help us see the values of others.

The Family: Sustaining, Passing, Responding

The impact of values and attitudes on the family was briefly addressed earlier in this chapter and highlighted the importance of viewing family roles and the assumption of authority or related practices. In most cultures, the family is considered the basic unit of society, and family structures are designed to support the particular needs of the group or culture. Values, roles and practices may vary, but most families maintain and pass on certain values, practices, traditions, and customs. The impact on families is greatest when factors like war, divorce, or catastrophic illness intervene or death separates the members of the family. The impact of preferences is felt when restrictions are placed on one or more members of the family without regard for their needs or when adherence to particular behavioral codes or practices inhibits their human development.

An article by Singular (1985) in *Empire Magazine* of the *Denver Post* illustrated the effect of transition from one culture to another and the impact on family values and work through a Hmong worker's description.

> Over there you had to go into a jungle, cut a tree and work very hard in raising chickens and all that just to eat. And you don't have a car and so many mosquitos come into your house. But even though it is a poor country I could take care of myself there.
> Here you work day-to-day and year-to-year and you worry too much about your job and you hurt and you're scared. (p. 21)

The impact of new values and preferences on this family's traditional cultural practices is revealed in this description of the Hmong worker's attempt to establish stability in a new land. In the same way values can be discovered in family experiences in a variety of areas. Look for values related to the cultural preferences of families in the following areas:

1. Festivals and celebrations

2. Religious practices

3. Social activities for women and for men

4. Job and career opportunities for women and for men

5. Dress restrictions for women and for men

6. Duties prior to marriage for women and for men

7. Distribution of financial responsibility

8. Restrictions regarding behavior

9. Permissions for marriage

10. Roles of family members

Religion

The impact of cultural preferences and values may be seen in the religious practices of a culture. These practices vary across cultures and may be related to the majority of customs observed within some cultures or to only a few of the customs in others; religious practices may even control customs in some. Major religions include Christianity, Judaism, Islam, Hinduism, Baha'i, Buddhism, Taoism, Shinto, Sikhism, Jainism, Confucianism, and Zoroastrianism and the many tribal religions of the world.

Although the majority of religions include music (usually group singing and instrumental), some do not. Participation may be individual, in small or large groups, formal or informal in structure, and focused on meditation and prayer or on study sessions.

Look for values related to the impact of preferences in religion in the following areas:

1. Religions represented in the culture

2. The presence of religion in government or in schools

3. Financial commitment of members

4. Numbers of members

5. Religious influence on the workplace

6. Interaction among members

7. Service to others

8. Religious restrictions or prohibitions

9. Religious leadership practices

10. Religious beliefs

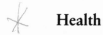 **Health**

The impact of preferences on health practices within cultures varies widely, from customs and practices focused on personal health to the treatment of illness or disease and concern for public areas. In most cultures the prevention of disease is a major concern. Practices and products, sanitation, and the care of self and others represent general concerns, as well.

Look for values related to the impact of preferences on health practices within a group or culture in the following areas:

1. Prevention of disease: immunization, diet, potable water, clean air

2. Treatment of disease: medication and treatment methods, facilities

3. Control of disease

4. Cleansing of the body

5. Practices for mental health

6. Financial support and plans

7. Care of the dead

8. Public facilities: toilets, bathing, transportation, streets

9. Control of, immunization of, removal of wastes for animals

10. Treatment of and support system for the physically, mentally, or emotionally impaired

Status and Relationships

The impact of values and preferences on the stratification of relationships within a particular group or culture varies widely but is felt in all cultures. Power and privilege or praise are visible marks of status and these manifestations may range from the awarding of an extra cow to personal selection as leader of a country. The conferring of status through a ritual focused on internal change may or may not be witnessed by others but may be found in the religious practices of most cultures.

Look for values related to the impact of preferences on status practices within an international community in the following areas:

1. Family

2. National government

3. Schools

4. Religious groups

5. Organizations

6. Military organizations

7. Universities

8. Business and industry

9. Local government

10. Awards and recognitions

Use of Time

The impact of values and preferences on the use of time within cultures may frequently pass unnoticed or unfelt, but it is worthy of consideration. The use of time, as with the other areas of impact (i.e., family, religion, health, and status relationships) varies across and within groups and cultures. As with the variations in the other categories, variations in the use of time may affect intercultural interaction and relationships.

The impact of the use of time by individuals and groups is felt, for example, when a training session scheduled to begin at 9:00 a.m. cannot begin until 9:30 a.m. because the participants haven't yet arrived. The impact of time related factors is felt when deadlines for a project have been set and the project is due but is, as yet, unfinished.

The kinds of time have been described by Hall (1989) as biological, personal, physical, metaphysical, micro (monochronic and polychronic), sync, sacred, profane, and meta. A review of these descriptions reveals differing concepts of time that you should be alert to in intercultural relationships:

- *Biological Time*: Time that was from the beginning; periodic, rhythmic; related to the biological clocks of living organisms; evidenced in jet lag
- *Personal Time*: The way in which people experience the flow of time; varies in different settings or conditions; evident in time-stood-still or time-flew-by feelings
- *Physical Time*: Time related to the movements of the sun; enabled people to start counting the days; evident in calculations for planting and harvesting and the positioning of sighting points throughout the world
- *Metaphysical Time*: Intimate time beyond the physical; unexplained theoretically but experienced personally; evident in deja vu experiences
- *Micro Time*: Culture-specific time evidenced in two patterns: monochronic (one-thing-at-a-time) time and polychronic (several-things-at-a-time) time

- *Sync Time*: Synchronized movements with time; evident in responses of infants to the human voice
- *Sacred Time*: Mythic, imaginary time; unchanging; story-like; evident in the feeling of "flowing with time"
- *Profane Time*: Time marking minutes, hours, days, months, years, decades, and centuries
- *Meta Time*: An abstraction regarding time discerned from temporal events based on all that has been written and said about time

Depending on the values of a culture, one or more of these forms of time may be evident in the lives of the people. Look for values related to the impact of preferences on the use of time within groups or cultures in these areas:

1. The ebb and flow of the tides

2. Meditation

3. Landmarks at fixed sites marking the sun's movement

4. Rituals and experiences or reports of metaphysical experiences

5. Variations in patterns of individual and group response to schedules

6. Observations of "time-bound" or "time-loosed" cultures in regard to the use of time

7. Music "in sync" with the movement of films; people dancing with music

8. Sacred ceremonies

9. The Julian Calendar

SUMMARY

Understanding the relationship of cultural values to attitudes and preferences is significant for personal skill development. The approaches presented here are designed to help you identify your learning needs related to valuing, to access appropriate resources, to practice needed skills, and to evaluate your learning. Whatever your present needs or roles, take a few moments to compare the components of your framework for action with the valuing-related components presented in this chapter and select any needed additions.

CHAPTER 4

Observing

Valuing has been described in the last chapter as the art of sensing, feeling and knowing certain acts, customs, and institutions in an especially favorable way. The focus of the chapter was on the important skills that you would need in order to function effectively in intercultural settings when people of varying backgrounds evidenced varied values. When considered together, the emphasis of the next five chapters should be described as focusing on the art of performing. Understanding differing ways of observing, listening, thinking, speaking, and gesturing represents a skill area of importance because these are areas common to all people in all cultures; recognition of the varied ways cultures perform, as well as understanding cultural variations in valuing, is an essential part of the framework for action presented in this book.

The art of observing is reviewed in this chapter with particular emphasis on observation of the immediate environment. Patterns of observation are included with emphasis on similarities and differences across cultures. Other areas of consideration include sites, people and objects, textures, movements, positions, and relationships.

CLOSE OBSERVATION: WHOLES AND PARTS

The ability to see total "pictures" and the relationship of parts of pictures to the whole may be one of the most commonly underdeveloped skills of learners. Because successful intercultural interaction is an ongoing learning process, the lack of this skill may inhibit the process. The world can be viewed as a "whole," with countries, cultures, and people seen as "parts." Countries can be viewed as wholes with people and cultures viewed as parts and a particular local area or its people or sites or customs might be seen as wholes with component parts. The problem is not that this imaging is so difficult. The problem is that seeing wholes and parts is an ability taken for granted and overlooked in most approaches to skill development.

The ability to see both wholes and parts may be overlooked because daily practice is necessary if it is to be used to achieve more successful intercultural communication. In a rapidly changing world of busy people going about their daily business in a frenzy of activity, time *is* a deterrent. However, for some of us, taking time to observe and seeing wholes and parts may be the first step toward achieving success in intercultural relations.

The Immediate Environment

You can see wholes and parts in your immediate environment, and one "whole" might be relationships. The nature of relationships has been addressed in earlier chapters dealing with your learning needs and it is seen in three important relationships: the relationship of the individual to the group, the relationship between adults and youth, and the relationship between males and females. Other relationships can and should be observed in a casual or informal way. These relationships are seen in daily life as part of the activity around us at home, at work, at recreational sites, and at places of worship. The ability to see these relationships should not be reserved for anthropologists, educators, psychologists, social scientists, and others whose work is related to close observation. These relationships can be recognized by people in day-to-day interaction and exchanges.

People and their interaction should be the first area of attention, not only because others are usually a part of our daily environments, but because people are capable of relating to each other and these relationships are observable (Galloway, 1971). People also relate to the environments in which they find themselves. That is, they relate to the **things** in a particular area as well as to other people. These relationships should also be noted in order to develop a more complete understanding of "people" relationships.

Cultural Patterns: People and Things

Consider, for example, the relationship between children on a playground and the recreational equipment available to them or people worshiping and their relationship to the site or to particular objects within the site. Consider people in any office and how they relate to the total environment: their relationship to the space, desks, files, typewriters, computers, copy machines, light fixtures, floor coverings, seats, charts, and other equipment or objects.

A weaver relates to the loom, the shuttles, the cloth to be woven, the patterns to be followed, and the yarn to be used. A spinner relates to space, the wheel or hand spindle, wool, hand carding items, and the spun yarn.

The tennis player not only relates to the other player or players, but to the net, and the court, balls, scoreboards, backstops and space. In their homes, people are seen not only in relationship to each other, but to the general and specific areas of space within the home: furniture, walls, ceilings and floor; plants and flowers or animals; windows, doors, and other items within the living area. People dining are seen (from our viewpoint and from their viewpoint, as well) in relation to the table, chairs, silverware, dishes, glasses and cups, food, table coverings, space, and structure surrounding them.

The concept of people relating to things may be bothersome to some of us if we view the concept as reducing the **status** of people in relation to things or as reduction of the status of one group by another. It is important to remember here that people **are related to things and to us**, that we **are related—to them and to things**—when we are present in a particular environment together. If status is a concern, it pertains to reduction of our status as observers, since we are not directly involved in the activities or interaction (if any) taking place. Observation of people in relation to things is important to an understanding of how people of all cultures live, of their daily activities, of their work and play. If we are unaware of this relationship or do not consciously relate to things in our own environments, the concept may not seem important to us. The relationship between persons with hearing impairments and their hearing aids, however, may be very close and necessary for effective functioning or understanding during the completion of daily activities. Even the terms that express our feelings of closeness are readily understood. Expressions such as "my own words" or "our own language" are commonly used.

In many cultures, people are consciously aware of the importance of relating to their environments. Interaction with the earth, sky, air, water, and space around them is as important as interaction with the structures within which they live, work, and learn or play. People in these cultures consciously recognize their relationship to these "things" and often **feel** directly related, expressing these feelings as "one-ness," a feeling of "connection" which may extend beyond the person's or group's physical state to the spiritual level, an experience of "connection" with God.

This "connection" is seen in cultures that consciously relate people to others, to earth and to sky, or to water or to nature because the spiritual and God are there. Through connection, they **experience** at-oneness. This experience is not to be seen as a mental or cognitive deduction, based on the observation of an assumed relationship, but as a felt, actual, and active relationship, a relationship between physical, spiritual, and inanimate objects in a world together. You should observe the parts, the "things," in the environment, and the meaning they have for the culture you are learning about.

Cultural Patterns: People and Events

This feeling of connectedness is shared between peoples and transmitted to succeeding generations through the various rituals and ceremonies which are repeated again and again throughout the years. Often the formats are highly organized and complex with full participation by members of the groups or of particular cultures. These rituals and ceremonies may serve to elevate the status of some or all of the participants or to reinforce the channels and bonds of connectedness. They enable members of the groups to openly express respect, gratitude, joy, or sadness, and to experience celebration in relation to the event. The relationship between people and events is an important relationship unto itself.

People relate directly to events and this relationship can be readily observed in religious events and other celebrations. In this relationship, the people are not only related to each other but to the various aspects of the event: the music, candlelight, special dances, food, drink, clothing, and focus or object of the event. This combination of elements produces responses that may vary in intensity at physical, emotional, mental, and spiritual levels. The responses may be visible and recognized by others or invisible and unrecognized. Responses may be focused only on the individual involved or on the group as a whole. In this individual-group relationship, at-oneness may be the goal. This experience is often described as a "spirit of community" or relatedness to the total group in celebration. The relationship is physical and spiritual; it is of the body and of the spirit or soul of the individuals involved.

It is in these gatherings within all cultures that one may witness an aspect of time referred to in the chapter on valuing. In religious gatherings, in particular, individuals may experience the feeling of sacred time (Hall, 1989). That is, the person may feel totally involved in the "flow" of time, as though time were a river and the person at-one with the movement. These experiences have been described by some as "having been a part of time." The experience of "flowing" with time in a ritual or celebration should not be confused with, although it is akin to, the feeling of "lost time" or "forgotten time" described in Chapter 3. This feeling may be expressed by the weaver, for example, or by a person involved in a creative project who "loses a sense of time."

These feelings are often expressed in creative settings, so often that creative people have frequently been described as "having no sense of time" when involved in creative endeavors of choice. In other words, their "clocks" appear stopped to persons around them and, later, to themselves.

Observations of people and events would be incomplete without recognition of the influence of a part of the event on the whole—music, for example. At a concert, individuals may be observed relating to the music and to various instruments as well as to the people and to the setting. Musicians and persons attending the concert may appear focused as though others around them were absent or they may show a minimal awareness of the presence of others. These relationships can be observed. A particular musician may touch or hold the instrument in a way that might be described as gently, tenderly, or even lovingly. The heads, arms, fingers, legs, or bodies of musicians may rotate or move in swaying, often trance-like ways, with eyes partially or fully closed. They may appear "under the spell of the moment" as though time were suspended for them.

On the other hand, musicians may appear ready to "push" time in a "move-it! move-it!" manner. This musician-music relationship is readily seen in rock concerts when music and body movements are more exaggerated, forceful, and intense. As the volume of the music increases, the motions of the musicians increase and movements of the musicians suggest that they own the space around them as they change positions and quicken or sustain various motions.

In the cases described above, musicians and their instruments may be described as "in-tune" in the figurative sense. Appearances of suspension or removal—from everyone and everything except the instrument—must not present the illusion that they are experiencing time as "flow" or forgotten and "lost." Their "in-tuneness" and their use of the instrument are in sync time (Hall, 1989). Body movements and manipulation of the instrument are synchronized to the beat or timing and length of the music. The universality of music and the diversity of individual expression or response to music not only demonstrates the relationship between commonality and diversity but offers a ready source of observation opportunities for you to view important cultural relationships.

Close observation of wholes and parts, of relationships between events and people, of relationships between people and things, or of relationships between people can help you understand intercultural interaction. Values and clues to the behavior of people are observable in interaction.

Observation of the relationship of people to action and to particular types of action is also helpful in skill building. People relate to activities as the musician relates to an instrument. That is, much can be learned from the relationship of an individual or a group to particular activities and events. Be particularly observant of the **parts** of a culture, the activities and events that are significant, as you work to gain understanding for more effective intercultural communication.

Cultural Patterns: People and Activities

Observation of any activity must not only include a focus on what is happening but on how it is happening. What is said may be as important as what is done; what is *not* done may be even more important. This means a close observer will look at the activities in which people are engaged, at the arrangements and interaction of people in the total setting, and at what is occuring in small groups. The movement of individuals, the patterns of movement within the total group, and the movement of the group as a whole are observable. The relationship of people to each other, the actions of individuals, and the patterns of conversation help us see the values and customs of a people and to begin to understand their behavior.

The problem is, as we attempt to observe others in group activities all of us have our preferences, based on our own values, and we all have an assortment of related and unrelated needs and skills (Oberg, 1972)—unrelated, that is, to the situation at hand. We tend to rely on what usually works well for us, or is of interest to us, and to avoid (consciously or unconsciously) engaging in activity that does not work well for us or that is of little interest to us. We may avoid conscious observation and then find that our developing understanding of a culture is not meeting our expectations; We may then begin to wonder why. When what we expected doesn't happen, and when what we expected to do isn't done, we probably need to take a closer look at ourselves in relation to the activity.

Be aware of the activities of a people in order to see the patterns which come together to develop, from many parts, the whole of their culture.

Cultural Patterns: People and Learning

Learning settings and approaches vary across and within cultures but learning is common to all people, beginning before birth and continuing until death. We have, for this reason, incentive to review learning as an important activity of everyday living.

Learning for adults may be formal or informal, structured or less structured, directed by the individual or directed by others. Viewed as "change," learning is seen to occur all around us, in our own environment and in the environments of others. For most adults, learning is voluntary; for others, learning may be a required activity. The needs, abilities, interests, attitudes, and styles of learners are reflected in the ways they relate to learning. Learning is personal.

When adult learners are closely related to learning, they are found to have a relationship like that of the musician with the instrument or that of the creative weaver with the loom. They are actively engaged: enthusiastic, productive, focused, self-directed, and eager to apply their learning (Knowles, 1980). These characteristics may not be so readily observed if the content of learning is incompatible with their needs, if their attitudes are not positive toward the learning, or if abilities and learning styles are not effectively matched to the learning. Whether or not the learning is voluntarily pursued is also an important factor that influences the response of the learner. For our purposes, consideration of the subject of learning styles is important in developing observation skills, with recognition of learning needs and attitudes as reviewed earlier.

People bring their own values, attitudes, preferences, knowledge, and roles to the learning setting. They also bring their physical conditions and assorted skills. All of these factors influence their ability to learn and they contribute to the creation of what is generally acknowledged as their "learning styles" (McCarthy, 1980).

Learning styles not only vary among individuals and groups within a culture but across cultures. These styles are seen in an individual's preference for learning through writing or illustrating or reading or listening. Learning style variations are often evident in the choices that people make between visual, oral, tactile, or aural methods. They are reflected in the learner's preferences for video tapes or movies, for example, rather than for lectures in the learning setting. Other learners may prefer discussion.

Individual learning styles are noted as learners employ approaches that are related to "feeling," "thinking," or "doing" levels. Learning styles also influence individual decisions to work alone or with a small or larger group. Some learners prefer to approach learning from a theoretical or abstract level (Kolb, 1983), to learn what others have learned and reported and to experience applied meaning later. Other learners prefer to learn from their experiences and to determine the meaning later.

These individual styles may appear similar in a particular group or culture and may be encouraged or nourished by that society. Particular preferences and the related skills may be highly developed and shared among members of the group or culture and passed to succeeding generations. Examples of this tradition-sharing can be seen in the pottery of cultures which continue to produce pottery in the shapes and designs that are unique to the particular culture. The members of these groups produce art, jewelry, cloth, and other products that are distinctively their own. In many cultures, men and women carry on these traditions according to gender, women producing particular items and men producing others.

The learning styles of a group are also reflected in the categories of products produced. Often categories may be determined by the materials at hand, but styles are reflected in *how* the materials are used. For example, art may be created instead of functional items or functional items instead of art.

Examples of cultural learning styles may be observed in cultures that produce significant numbers of philosophers or opera singers or artists or lawyers or engineers or, as indicated above, potters. Could the preferences be based on precedence or role modeling rather than learning styles? Perhaps; but preparation for professions requires learning and the ability to perform, and learning styles influence the manner in which learning is acquired.

Whatever the reason (or combination of reasons) for learning, the degree to which learners relate to learning is worthy of consideration in understanding relationships. The relationship between individuals and groups of individuals or activities may be culturally reflected in learning settings and is observable. Watch the ways in which members of a culture typically learn; that is one of the parts that makes up the whole of their common experience. The more clearly you understand these parts, the more clearly you will understand the whole.

Cultural Patterns: People and Work

The work place is a source of observables for noting the relationship of people to work. Work settings vary widely across cultures with wide variations in individual responses and abilities to relate effectively (Kolb, 1983). As in the learning setting, persons bring their own needs and preferences, knowledge, roles, and styles to the setting. These styles may be learning and work related. Satisfied employees, too, exhibit enthusiastic, focused productivity, productivity that, if not entirely self-directed, is participative and supportive of the established direction. These characteristics may not be so readily observed if the nature of the work or the rewards are incompatible with personal needs, if attitudes are not positive toward the work, or if abilities and work styles are not effectively matched to the work.

The structure, appearance, and organization of work sites

may influence the degree to which the employee is able to relate to the site and to the people in the environment. Our focus, however, must be the relationship of the person to the work. To what degree does the employee or worker enjoy or register dissatisfaction with the work experience? How does the person respond to the duties assigned? What is the nature of the work? Is the work performed alone or with others? Are the duties generally recognized as important? To what degree? What skills are necessary? What levels of performance are required? How is the work evaluated? Are benefits attached to performance? Is the worker compensated? Does the worker want to continue performing the duties?

These and other questions should be addressed in order to understand the relationship between the person and work.

Dissatisfaction with work may be expressed in observable ways and should be distinguished from satisfaction related to the work setting or to the people or other factors in the work environment. For example, the person may be pleased during interaction with the people in the environment and dissatisfied with the work or may enjoy the monetary compensation and dislike the work.

Attitudes may influence responses (Korten, 1976). Within and across cultures people may be observed to continue the tasks assigned—alone or with others—with negative relationship to the work itself. However, whatever the nature of the person's relationship to work, it is possible to see the influence of values and culture.

Evidence of negative person-work relationships is frequently found in cultures where racial-ethnic, religious, or gender-related practices affect individuals or groups within the culture and in the workplace. In these cultures, discriminatory practices and stereotypes serve to project an image of reduced status and humanity, and persons are relegated to lower positions on work and social scales.

In determining the relationship of persons to work in these settings or conditions, you will need to observe the areas described, to obtain related resources, and to become proficient at comparing and contrasting relationships. The determination of similarities and differences in relationships can be challenging. For example, it must not be assumed that persons are satisfactorily related to work when they appear content but cannot or may not obtain other work. A positive relationship between the person and work must not be presumed when gender inequity is present. People may relate in order to eat but the relationship may be considered negative.

The work of a people is a very important part of the people's whole cultural identity. It is necessary to understand their relationship to that work in order to understand and communicate with them effectively.

Cultural Patterns: People and Travel

The relationship of people to travel is an area that should be addressed as you work to establish a practical framework for action. Travel offers a rich source of opportunities for the observation of relationships: commonality and diversity, the individual and the group, and wholes and their parts. People can and do relate to the travel experience and this relationship can be observed.

The relationship of people to travel can be observed in all parts of the world and patterns are as diverse as they are in other relationships. Throughout the world, travel is possible by foot, bicycle, boat, motorcycle, car, cart, bus, train, plane, ship, or other less recognized mode. The relationship of people to travel should be recognized because travel as an activity requires effective skills on the part of the persons involved if the relationship is to be successful. You can use travel as a valuable learning resource.

Many factors make travel an experience of discovery because the nature of travel is observably dimensional. That is, the experience requires people to relate to factors that may or may not be a part of their prior experiences and that they may or may not be adequately prepared to encounter. Transportation, interaction, and eating, resting, housing, and financial factors must be addressed. Questions related to health, language, customs and practices, religious facilities, and other concerns must be considered (Oberg, 1972). Finally, the needs, preferences, skills, and roles you pack with other belongings must go along, and your values will go along as well! Traveling with your values can be a challenge!

Travel, too, can be a satisfying or disappointing experience and the degree to which you relate to diversity may be positive or negative. Positively related travelers evidence enthusiasm, openness to discovery, the ability to interact successfully, and flexibility. These persons may vow to return, to explore new areas, to learn a language, or to look for alternatives when plans must be changed. These people can be found across the world and within all cultures—smiling or learning, practicing skills or reading books in airports.

Dissatisfaction with travel is also expressed in observable ways but must be distinguished from dissatisfaction with other elements or factors that might influence the individual's personal response. For example, people often travel to get away from something in their own local environments. Their immediate goal may or may not be the destination. Frequently, persons travel abroad involuntarily and may not be excited about the prospect; they did not make the decision to go. In these situations, travel is viewed negatively **before** the activity begins!

Dissatisfaction is usually related to one or more of the factors mentioned earlier: personal needs, preferences, skills, or roles. Dissatisfaction may be expressed if persons are accustomed to particular personal practices that are not a part of the new area or if they are uncomfortable with people from a wide variety of backgrounds or if they cannot communicate effectively.

Dissatisfaction with food, health practices, religion, or social customs is observable and dissatisfaction with forms of communication or available services is observable. You will be able to determine an individual's relationship to travel through these areas of observation. And although response to travel and to interaction with other cultures may be an individual's personal response, it is likely to reflect a reaction to change from the person's own cultural background, as well. Recognition of this fact will help you to more effectively understand, and thus communicate with, the individual.

Cultural Patterns: Group Movement

Reference has been made to the need for close observation in the local environment with particular attention to the relationship of individuals to the group and their interaction or activities. Observations of patterns of conversation should include what is said and what remains unaddressed—from your viewpoint, what might have been included.

Conversation between group members does "move" the group in another, but very real, sense. This "movement" can be observed in the amount of verbal exchange, laughter, and joking and in the numbers of persons involved in the exchange. For example, groups observed as "noisy" usually involve many people speaking or laughing or engaged in animated verbal exchange at the same time. They are seen to be moving rapidly from subject to subject and their conversation may be accompanied by observable physical activity for example (gestures or facial and body movements).

"Quiet" groups may or may not involve many people engaged in verbal exchange at the same time. They usually move less rapidly from topic to topic, however, and exhibit less physical activity.

When one individual speaks or when conversation is limited to a few persons, groups may exhibit little verbal or physical movement. Movement increases as the number of involved participants increases.

Patterns of conversation vary among cultures and will be addressed in Chapter 7. Here, it is important to realize that verbal exchange is valued highly in some cultures and less in others. Some individuals, too, may be inclined to speak more frequently than others. Knowledge of the language may be an important influencing factor under certain circumstances or hesitancy to use the language may be an influencing factor in others. In some cases, others may choose not to be involved in conversation because it is not their "style."

Verbal exchange does influence the movement of individual and group thoughts, however, and these patterns are discernible (Hall, 1969). For example, particular individuals may initiate conversation with many others, moving about the group easily and freely; others may position themselves in relation to one or several others during an entire event. Small groups may form and discussion or laughter may accompany the interaction of a particular group. The "tone" of a group is expressed in observable ways and may be just as distinct as that of an orchestra. Your ability to discover patterns of conversation and verbal exchange among persons of the same and of different cultures will increase your understanding of similarities and differences and enable you to adjust your own behavior as desired. Most of us don't want to sound our tubas when our flutes are required.

It is important to note the "tone" of the group in terms of the values of the group rather than in terms of your own values. For example, if the group appears to interact quietly by your own standards, you may need to observe interaction over a period of time to arrive at a conclusion. The group may, indeed, be quiet by your standards but you are interested in observing through their standards, not yours, and a brief period of observation may be inadequate for your purposes. The amount of verbal interaction often reflects group values and you will need a broader time frame to determine cultural values.

Negative group movement may also be observed in verbal exchanges. That is, the group may fail to exchange information as it regularly does because of negative input, internal or external influences that interfere with verbal expression. A status figure may appear, for example, and a "hush" may come over the group. Offensive language may be introduced, or one or more members may dominate during the interaction.

Group "movement" may also be observed in the observation of unspoken exchanges, non-verbal expressions such as facial or body movements that indicate displeasure, pleasure, or anger. Smiles, the placement of hands on hips, departures from the group, or other "statements" received from group members can influence group dynamics.

Non-verbal exchanges are important in group relationships because these expressions, too, reflect values, preferences, and styles. They also enable persons to understand each other when the languages are not common. Non-verbal exchanges and gesturing are addressed in Chapter 8.

Observation of the individual parts of group interaction may provide the observer with many hints about the culture of the participants of the group.

Cultural Patterns: Thing-To-Thing Relationships

The relationship of inanimate objects or "things" to other objects is another important area of observation. Just as people relate to things or objects, objects may be observed in relation to each other. Recognition of this relationship is important in intercultural communication because it enables us to see the values, preferences, and skills of the particular group or culture.

The skill of creating relationships among objects is highly developed in some cultures and highly prized. Natural objects—rocks, bark, wood, fibers, plants, flowers, or trees—are often used to symbolize particular relationships or concepts and beliefs or to create relationships between people and the objects. Space may be considered in an arrangement and viewed in its own configuration around, or in relation to, the particular objects (Edwards, 1979). For example, the space around a picture may be viewed in relation to the picture, just as the picture may be viewed in relation to the space.

In addition to space and the particular objects, textures and colors or shapes and sizes of the objects may be considered. We are viewed as related to the items, just as they are viewed as related to us and to each other. Observation of the relationships of objects to objects, or of people to objects or activities or time may help us relate to each other in effective intercultural interaction—where our values show. Each of these parts, each of these cultural patterns, comes together to create the whole cultural experience.

This might be the time for you to reflect on the examples of observable relationships presented in this chapter so far and for you to determine how these components can fit into your action framework.

The External Environment

The external environments of people influence their interaction and reflect their values just as their internal environments do. These external environments include public areas, buildings, sculpture and art, signs and roads, or elements of the landscape. The positions of these elements, their formats and relationships, must also be considered in discerning the values of the people being observed.

Cultural Patterns: Values and Color

Artists and others have realized the relationship of people to color. We speak of color values and "matching" accessories; of matching color of skin, hair, or eyes to particular colors; or of "my color" when related to clothing. We add color to our skin or nails or hair. We consider color "warm" or "cool" as though it were part of us. Our feelings are related to colors—the colors of living things and of daily objects.

Color is an important element in the external environment as well, when relationships are considered. We borrow from the environment to create our descriptions and assign color as well as tonality to our descriptions of the environment. A fabric may have "earth tones," for example; a lake may be "azure blue," a field of wheat "bright golden"; the exterior of a building may be viewed as exhibiting "somber tones of gray."

These culture-specific descriptions may be readily understood in the United States and may be similarly understood or interpreted in many other national cultures. It is important to note, however, that the meaning of "earth tones," for example, may vary across cultures according to the type of earth present and the tonalities of color that are familiar to the people. In intercultural settings, the close observer must not only be consciously aware of personal descriptions or interpretations but also be open to the descriptions and interpretations of others, in this case, open to their interpretations concerning color but also open to their interpretations concerning other relationships described in this chapter.

Cultural Patterns: Values and Structures

Shapes and sizes of buildings are another important area of consideration in the external environment. The architecture of an area reveals special values related to a particular culture and these values may be especially visible in structures associated with religious practices: churches, mosques, synagogues, temples, cathedrals and simple shrines or places of worship. Schools and office buildings or museums are additional areas of special interest. Concert halls or cabins and restaurants or old and new structures may represent only the beginning of a rich resource base.

Values are reflected, too, in the textures present in the external environment: smooth or rough stones of structures; grassy and concrete areas; zones of sand, earth or water; areas of bark and leaves. Learning to recognize the relationship of people to these external elements of their environments is a necessary skill. The recognition of these relationships enables us to acknowledge, to understand, and to respect these elements of their environments as well as of our own.

One of the most important parts of the external environment is the home. A structure demonstrating duality, the home is at once a personal part of the internal environment for the occupants and a public part of the external environment for others. Just as houses demonstrate duality, they also represent cultural diversity. Houses in a particular area of the world may include shrines. Homes from other areas may be arranged by the layout of rooms to indicate parental authority with sites for sons by birth order or with sites arranged to indicate the relative status of males and females. Other homes are designed to maintain visual privacy but to enable occupants to hear the activities of others.

Provision of bathing and toilet facilities may vary from modern to simple, requiring the use of a nearby river or canal (Oberg, 1972). Houses may be owned by occupants or relatives, contain a great deal or a minimum of furniture, and be structured to accommodate traditional or extended family systems. A home may be made of a variety of materials or be designed as an open structure.

Homes reflect the cultural values of a people and an understanding of this relationship is important to understanding the relationships of people to things and the relationship of things to other things. As part of a particular community, houses not only "speak" nonverbally of those within but of the values of their culture (Bochner, 1973). Houses may even be necessary to a culture's continuing expression: old houses bring an awareness of the past to present generations.

SUMMARY

The ability to see wholes and parts of wholes and to relate the meaning of these discoveries to human values is a necessary skill for persons desiring to improve their intercultural interaction and communication. The ability to recognize the varied ways in which people relate to things and the relationship between objects or things helps us understand our world.

CHAPTER 5

Listening

The primary focus of this chapter deals with listening patterns and cultural variations. Primary areas of consideration include variations in types of listening, frequency and duration of listening patterns, and active and passive approaches.

In Chapter 4, close observation was suggested as a window to understanding the culture and values of a people and was presented as a skill area to be developed. Listening to the conversation of people was one of the ways suggested for building understanding. Developing the habit of listening may be difficult for people who are part of highly verbal cultures and who value verbal exchange in interaction, as well as for persons whose preferred learning style is verbal exchange. Listening may also be difficult for individuals who value brief or rapid verbal exchanges during interaction. When the levels of aural tolerance have been reached for these people, they may become uncomfortable with language as a preferred method of communication. They may prefer to do things quickly; they may prefer only brief periods of listening. In addition, while other people usually want to talk, patterns vary, and this variety may signal the need for flexibility on the part of the listener if effective interaction is to be achieved. Thus, to develop effective intercultural communication, you must be aware of your own listening style and you must be alert to the culturally influenced listening styles of others.

ACTIVE LISTENING

In considering your own listening style the distinction should be made between hearing or "receiving" words and listening to words. The relationship of hearing words and listening is similar to that of the knowledge and understanding levels discussed earlier. Hearing words is at the knowledge level and listening is at the understanding level. To make sense with words, they must be **related** to something—a concept, an experience, a person, a value—to establish meaning. To establish meaning, a person must be able not only to hear, but to listen. The ability to listen actively is especially important in intercultural settings because information must be clearly transmitted and received if understanding is to occur, even when an understanding of the language is not a barrier to communication.

Interviews

Although diverse in approach and content, some form of interview process is common to most cultures. Because the process demands listening skills as well as the ability to question creatively, interviews present an opportunity for you to develop listening skills within and outside of your own culture.

Persons interviewing across cultures will find it helpful to observe the commonly accepted approaches to interviewing within a new culture before using their own familiar procedures. Attention should be given specifically to practices related to formality, questioning, and conversational patterns. For example, consider appropriate dress, roles of the interviewer and the interviewee, courtesies and status relationships, and length of the interview. The length of an interview may even be determined by how people of the local culture regularly engage in conversation or business practices.

In intercultural settings where language presents a barrier to communication qualified interpreters should be involved in the interview process since clarity and understanding are required. The ability to listen actively, however, remains a priority for an effective interviewer.

Marlene Wilson (1983, p. 123) has described the qualities of an effective interviewer and the common errors that may be made in the interview process. The "ability to listen attentively and hear accurately" is in the list of effective qualities she identified. In the list of errors, she notes additional key factors: "making decisions too early in the interview" and "letting pressure of duties shorten the interview time." An interviewer cannot carry out the decision-making process effectively without **relating** what is heard and cannot relate information if the absence of sufficient time interferes with the acquisition process. Thus an interviewer who values brief, "get to the point" interpersonal communications must be alert to an interviewee who is culturally oriented toward a more leisurely interview process.

Many times an interview has become a disappointment because an interviewer had not taken time and listened to the person being interviewed or the person had not taken time and listened to what the interviewer was saying, had not **really** heard. For example, the work place may become the site of difficult interaction when the topic is performance and the employee does not know what or how to perform because he or she had not listened well or long enough to understand what was said. Persons applying for jobs or conducting interviews in intercultural settings must not only develop effective listening skills but should be prepared to work harder at the task. Patience and commitment will be required to understand the interviewing practices of the local culture and to achieve successful interaction.

Group Action

Speech patterns are one of the many observables in group interaction and you must utilize the skill of listening if group interaction and movement is to develop into effective intercultural communication. As mentioned earlier, it is important to observe who speaks and what is said, for these factors influence group movement. Listening helps you identify what is said and relate it to roles. For example, the blocker who argues and rejects ideas can be readily identified. It is interesting to note that common descriptions of group roles focus on the use of speech to assist or to interfere with the progress of the group because speech is such an important observable. The effective listener must listen closely enough to what is said to be able to distinguish between persons aiding or interfering with the progress of the group. The following questions should be answered:

1. Who seeks or offers information?

2. Who proposes tasks or goals or defines problems?

3. Who offers suggestions or ideas or alternatives?

4. Who argues, criticizes, or blames?

5. Who interrupts or attempts to speak for others?

6. Who whispers?

7. Who boasts or seeks recognition through exaggerations?

The answers to these and other related questions can only be found by listening closely during interaction.

The art of listening in group behavior can be helpful in identifying the patterns of leadership. These patterns can be recognized by what leaders say. Listening and leadership patterns vary across cultures and determining leadership through observing speech patterns demands close listening skills. For example, it is necessary for an effective listener to be able to distinguish between the leader who tells the group what to do and the leader who persuades the group to take certain action, or to note the leader who asks for reactions and involves members of the group actively. Individual and cultural values will influence the patterns preferred, of course, and these values can be discerned through listening.

Active listening at international work sites is especially important. We need to become aware of the values of the people around us and these are often revealed more quickly and with less opportunity for failure if we look and listen **first**. Individuals from cultures where highly verbal communication is valued may find it difficult to listen, and this pattern can be a problem in many situations and especially so in consulting projects.

Helen Clinard (1985, p. 39) has described the difficulty of listening: "The assumption that you already know how to listen is the biggest barrier to improving listening skills." For the individual or consultant desiring to develop more effective listening skills, Clinard suggests that reading about skills is not enough: "Increasing your listening skills will require practice and self-discipline. It is not easy, but the rewards are tremendous and come in many forms."

In explaining the importance of listening in an overseas setting, McCaffrey and Hafner (1985, p. 26) observed that a particular consultant abroad had been evaluated as highly successful because "The consultant asked appropriate questions in an unhurried way, listened intently and clarified what was said to make sure everyone understood."

The Family

The development of listening skills can begin in our own homes. Families are usually effective resources during the development of these skills. One reason is that we are highly verbal as a culture. The other reason is that everyday living sounds are a good place to begin to practice.

Family interaction is a resource for practice with the discovery of values through listening as well. One of the most frequent complaints women make is that "husbands don't listen" and men often answer "I don't have time" (Tannen, 1990). When children scream (literally) to be heard and parents both complain "You don't understand," it may be time to look at listening patterns and to improve skills. As an example of the ease in which potentially erroneous judgments can be made based on flawed listening, Tannen notes

When men do all the talking at meetings, many women, including researchers—see them as "dominating" the meeting, intentionally preventing women from participating, publicly flexing their higher-status muscles. But the **result** that men do most of the talking does not necessarily mean than men **intend** to prevent women from talking. (p. 95)

Tannen's observations were focused on public meetings, presumably of adults, but adult gender-related interaction and listening patterns can be observed in the family, as well. Frequently observation of the family offers an additional opportunity: the chance to observe both adult-youth and gender-related interaction and listening patterns.

Because the development of listening skills in the family can take place through regular interaction and experiences, you might wish to practice improving your listening skills by

- engaging in activities with a highly verbal child for three hours;
- listening to family members describe their special needs;
- listening to a member beyond the time you would prefer to listen; or
- listening for particular points to be made without interruption.

These activities may appear ordinary but habits are acquired through daily activities and our "habits" related to listening may be effective or inadequate for our purposes. Habits influence our skills and skills can be improved with practice.

The habit of listening can begin at home with others around you but also as you relate to the sounds inside and outside of the home. Your immediate environment can be the source of training for experiences abroad. Everyday living sounds should be seen as valuable resources, but they often pass unnoticed.

The importance of improving listening skills through the identification of common sounds has been described by Ricard (1978). Any ordinary sound can be a subject in your skill development: an airplane, a train, a fountain, or children singing, for example. The aim is to identify sources, to listen to the sound, and to listen long enough to identify other sounds around you.

Do you recognize the sound of chopping an apple on a wooden board? Of turning the pages of a book or entering items into a word processor? A carnival or festival offers many opportunities for discovering sounds.

While sound is significant as we develop listening skills, lack of sound is also significant. In highly verbal cultures, we may frequently be uncomfortable with silence. This discomfort may be observed through listening to common expressions of our culture:

- "I just didn't know what to say!"
- "I should have said something!"
- "I should have said *something*!"
- "It was awful! Nobody said a word!"

This tendency is illustrated when people feel the immediate need to respond to questions whether or not they want to answer or know the answer.

But silence, too, is around us to be explored. This discovery will serve us well during travel-related experiences within or outside of the United States. Pauses and silence are to be found in speech and silence is what makes speech speech or music music. Silence plus sound equals language; when they kiss, we hear music!

An appreciation for silence will help us develop listening skills and we must search for opportunities to be silent and **relate** to silence if our skills are to be improved. This means searching for the quiet places in our own environments, places that offer us the gift of silence or near silence, places without words. This means searching for the opportunity to hear nothing, or to hear just the chirp of an occasional cricket, a bird's call, or the sound of rustling leaves. We must search for opportunities to hear a baby's breath, a sigh, or the touch of a pen to paper. These may be moments to cherish, and through really hearing them our listening skills will improve rapidly. When our own listening skills are highly developed, it is possible for us to appreciate more fully the customs and practices of persons and cultures described as "quiet people," to recognize the sounds of a new culture that

are like and unlike those in our own, and to discover the value
of silence as realized by people of many cultures throughout the
world.

Music

Music offers us the opportunity to experience sound with
or without words. Preferences for music vary but any music will
enable us to practice our listening skills: classical, popular, jazz,
folk, rock, or bluegrass. Music also enables us to listen for variations in sound—the highs, the lows, the beat, the tones. When
listening, try to experience feelings (or to identify attitudes)
about or toward the music. How do you relate? Negatively or
positively? How do you account for this response? Are your values showing? These and other questions will help you understand
how individuals and cultures relate to music.

The relationship of a particular culture may be seen in the
words and the meaning of the music as well as in the rhythms.
Often the words may reflect the conditions, concerns, and needs
of the people. In "Understanding People Through Music,"
Jankovic and Edwards (1980) have described music that is not
developed commercially but that has been historically used to
express the human experience.

> It is not intended for a larger audience. The beauty of such music
> lies in its meaning for the performers and listeners, not in the
> sound per se.
> This music is usually locality-oriented and may range from sub-
> jects focused on health and work conditions to specific events that
> are familiar to the people of the area. (p. 5)

However, while the words of music may reflect conditions
they may also convey stereotypes; just as other media—newspa-
pers, television, movies—stereotype, music may use words that
describe the people, their area, or their activities in false ways.
Jankovic and Edwards (1980, p. 78) cautioned adult educators
who would be working within intercultural areas to "approach
the task, insofar as possible, without the conceived notions and

stereotypes which may have accumulated from their exposure to media portrayals." This caution might be offered to persons working in any intercultural setting and should include reference to the parameters of our own musical knowledge, experience, and preferences.

We may have a tendency to select music which is familiar to us and to listen only, or primarily, to this music. In the development of listening skills, it is well to select unfamiliar music that reflects the values of other individuals and cultures as well as our own (Feltz, 1975). Music is a tool for communication which is useful in transmitting messages across vast areas in many cultures by a variety of methods. Music can be used to discuss meanings of particular types. Social protest songs, love songs, or songs reflecting status relationships, for example, might be learning resources in a discussion group or in a formal classroom setting. Religious music is often a resource for discussions focused on the music of a particular group or culture. Music from different cultures can be the source of information regarding both particular musical systems and tastes.

Language

Language is helpful during the listening process, not only because it delivers words from which meaning can be derived, but because it illustrates regional variations in the use of the same language. A particular accent or variation of the stress, pitch, or tone of a syllable may be discovered through listening; it may be recognized as part of the **non-verbal** aspect of language. Regional dialects from within and outside of the United States serve as rich cultural resources for listening development.

FREQUENCY AND DURATION PATTERNS

Frequency patterns of the speech of individuals offer another area of observation that should be helpful during skill development. This area is often troublesome because of the variations in individual patterns (Tannen, 1990). "Some people ramble on and on," listeners may say, and the expression is not uncommon. "Make your point," say others, and this too is a common expression. When some people ramble or can't seem to make their points—at least from our viewpoint—it may help to look at what is reflected in their speech patterns. This subject will be addressed in Chapter 7. However, the implications for listening are of concern here.

When we believe a person rambles or can't get to the point, it is important to look at our own speech habits and preferences. How do we speak and for how long? Is our individual pattern culturally similar to or different from others in the target area? We are related to our language and preferences, and our values are reflected in these personal patterns. As with earlier observations, it is well to begin with understanding of ourselves in order to understand others. When we want to understand others, this approach usually helps.

If our speech is rapid and to the point, it would be easier for us if the speech patterns of others were similar. We could meet our goals in conversation and be on our way. If our speech patterns aren't similar to those of others with whom we must communicate, we do have choices. We might

- slow down,
- encourage others to speed up, or
- leave.

After acting on any of these choices we usually become frustrated. An alternative to becoming frustrated might be to **practice** slowing down (since the chances of getting others to speed up may be rather slim). During the practice period, we might become frustrated, but at least our frustration might not be viewed by others. This alternative is a win-win situation: We are spared frustration, gain a new skill, and—if we're lucky—gain insight into the values of others. Others can do what they do; they will appreciate our courtesy, and—if they're lucky—they will see the values we reveal. Our new skill can be used selectively, as needed, and we keep our own habit (which travels with us).

How often a person speaks, or doesn't speak, may also interfere with our ability to listen. If we are uncomfortable with silence or pauses, the waiting can be almost unbearable. Counselors and others who listen for a living will tell you that the art of listening must be developed to a high degree just to remain seated under certain circumstances. "Too fast" or "too slow" speech patterns that don't match our own can be trying in the listening process, trying to patience and to skill building as well.

Often, individuals and members of groups within a particular culture may be seen as "quiet people." These people can talk—and will, occasionally. In a listening situation with them the absence of sound may be a problem for some of us (but not for them) and we may have to decide what to do. We do have a choice. We might

- encourage them to talk
- talk for them
- squirm in our seats

or seek an alternative. For example, we might practice waiting to hear what they have to say. What do we have to lose? They use their preferred way of communicating; we learn a new skill, and (in our pockets) we retain our preferred way of communicating to use later. If we practice listening even when the delivery is not to our liking, we might learn. What do you think? The choice is yours.

CULTURAL PATTERNS AND VARIATIONS

Cultural patterns of listening vary among individuals within and across cultures. All cultures have customs, however, that should be observed in regard to listening and silence. In most cultures, there are sites, public or private, where silence must be observed and the ability to listen comfortably is required. Where gender related practices exist, for example, women may be required to be silent under particular circumstances. Children may also be required to maintain silence in compliance with existing customs. All people in all cultures maintain silence under particular conditions.

In some cultures, silence is to be maintained in the presence of older persons or persons in positions of authority or in the presence of the dead. These requirements may be imposed legally or simply may be generally accepted as traditional practices among the people.

Practices regarding silence in places of worship are seen to vary widely. In many religions, music may be common in the rituals or ceremonies, with group singing and choral and instrumental music. Other religions may forbid the use of music. Chants and dancing may or may not be a part of ceremonies and individuals may or may not pray aloud. In most ceremonies, there are periods of brief or extended silence. Persons leading the ceremonies may deliver spoken or sung messages as the assembled group remains silent or becomes periodically involved.

Mourning practices are similarly varied regarding individual and group responses to death. Practices usually include periods of silence in which respect is rendered to the departed person and to the person's spirit or soul. In many cultures, however, the rituals or ceremonies include prayers and incantations or audible expressions of grief that may be expressed by a number or by all of the persons assembled. Listening and learning can help us understand the meaning behind these practices.

Individuals and some cultures may appear to value noisy, animated interchange accompanied by bands, dancing, revelry, or singing. Others strive to maintain what might be described as a certain decorum that is observable in public and in private areas. You will discover these contrasts as you develop the necessary listening skills. Values and preferences will be visible and you will be able to compare your own for purposes of personal growth; your framework for action will be focused on personal learning needs.

Knowing where and when to listen is important and practice is essential, but it is equally important to be aware of several facts regarding the relationship of listening to space. Hall (1969) has described the space required for listening. He notes that the area effectively covered by the unaided ear is limited and reports the following:

1. Up to 20 feet: very efficient

2. At 100 feet: one-way vocal communication is possible

3. Beyond 100 feet: auditory cues break down (p. 42)

Some individuals and cultures are more sensitive to acoustic space (or sound in the atmosphere) than others and voices resounding in a cathedral, for example, may be considered annoying. It is possible for some individuals in some cultures to screen out particular sounds and to pay close attention to others. These patterns may be developed over a period of time and may remain fairly constant.

RESOURCES AND PRACTICES

In addition to areas of interaction, where conversations and sounds may be readily observed, the learner's attention should be directed toward the use of audio-visual media and computers as resources. Radio, television, audio-tapes, movies, and video tapes offer opportunities for observing and listening to intercultural exchanges. The radio and audio-tapes are especially helpful because the visual is screened and only the ears receive the messages. The audio-visual items are helpful because they represent the "picture" as in daily living interaction. One advantage of using audio and video-tapes (or any of the other items that you have ready access to) is that they offer you the opportunity to repeat the information during practice periods. These resources can be valuable, too, for learning a language. Differences between what is heard during interaction and what is heard when using tapes may be anticipated because in intercultural interaction individual speech patterns vary; you may also be exposed to accents or dialects present in the local environment.

Experienced travelers may be a special resource regarding active listening. Discussions with these travelers, within and outside of the United States, can help you understand the similarities among and differences between the people and cultures related to their travels.

PASSIVE LISTENING

Active listening skills and related knowledge areas have been the focus of the discussion above because the information is oriented toward success. Successful intercultural interaction is the goal of this text. The marks of passive listening, however, should be introduced so that you will recognize and avoid them when you are practicing.

Passive listening is observable when

1. A listener "hears" but does not "receive" the information

2. A listener is not attentive in a particular exchange

3. A listener does not allow enough time to listen

The relationship between listening, attention, and time must be recognized to improve listening skills, and passive listening interferes with and severs these essential connections. In successful intercultural communication, for example, we must be able to receive and relate information or ideas in order to understand. We must also be able to clarify, to confirm, or frequently to restate what is heard and then to pose questions. All of these procedures take time and demand our attention. Few of these processes result from passive listening.

More importantly, we must be able to learn from speakers in intercultural settings; we must be able to focus and to exchange. Passive listening will not achieve this desired end.

SUMMARY

As reviewed in this chapter, the art of listening must be practiced to be developed, wherever and whenever the opportunity is presented. You will need to compare the listening components of your original framework with the components presented in this chapter. Active at best, listening challenges us to receive and relate, to store and retrieve information effectively; these are essential skills for successful intercultural communication.

CHAPTER 6

Thinking

The focus of this chapter emphasizes the variation in thinking patterns and approaches to problem solving among people and how recognition of these similarities and differences can be a valuable tool for improving communication and interaction skills.

In Chapters 4 and 5, the primary focus of your skill building was on the development of observation and listening skills. This chapter will help you relate observation and listening to thought. Thinking is a complex process and our special need is to discover how thinking as a process is related to cultural similarities and differences and how this relationship influences intercultural interaction.

During your skill development and the completion of activities in this book, you will use all of the thinking patterns briefly described below and you will probably find one or more of the approaches related to your own cognitive style, the way you think best. Because thought cannot be separated from learning or its related approaches, or from the learner's particular needs and preferences, this chapter will address basic theoretical concepts underlying each of these areas. The ultimate goal of this chapter will be to help you understand the relationship of these concepts to thinking, your own skill development, and intercultural interaction. Information discussed in this chapter will be of special significance to individuals who serve as teachers, trainers, or facilitators for adults learning in an intercultural environment.

THOUGHT PATTERNS

Studies of thinking patterns note a number of cultural variations with some commonalities. An understanding of thought must include knowledge of brain, body, and emotional function and the relationship of these functions to the thinking process. For our purposes, however, a brief review of the thinking process and related patterns must be the primary focus. This approach is appropriate because the influence of brain hemispheric preferences on patterns of thought is observable. For our purposes, too, understanding of the relationship of the values represented in cultural patterns and practices is necessary for skill building. You will need to give special attention to your own understanding of this particular relationship, and the other relationships presented in this chapter, when comparing the components of your own framework for action with the components of the suggested framework.

Linear Thinking

Linear thinking, commonly associated with left hemispheric brain function, is often considered traditional or logical thinking. For some time, we believed that thinking should begin at one point and proceed to another, to still another and another, and, finally, should reach a point of conclusion. This linear, pencil-like process was translated into speech so that words, to make sense, should reveal this linear approach and "logically" present information in an idea-linked, linear exchange. This linear approach is seen in the sentence-based structure of this book and in the way all of us learned to take notes, a familiar, standard format.

Studies have indicated that the brain has the ability to think in nonlinear ways as well, to be more creative than ever before imagined; these studies have indicated that the brain establishes a variety of "patterns" before channeling them into the words that we exchange in linear fashion. This sorting and sifting of concepts, accomplished in the brain, is presumed to be achieved through a complex network of systems and released through words which have meanings of their own. These words may be misunderstood by the receiver who has an individual set of personal associations in the mind. In other words, a complex system of thought may be confined and restricted by the words we have selected to transmit thought and by the ways in which those words are understood by others. Thus, linear communication can be easily misunderstood among individuals with the same language and cultural backgrounds. How much more easily can linear thought be misunderstood by peoples of various cultures and backgrounds speaking different languages.

Lateral Thinking

Edward de Bono (1983) conceived the idea of lateral or parallel thinking as thinking related to the generation of new ideas and extending ideas through imagination. In his view, this type of thinking enables the person to arrive, through specific approaches, at diverse sets of conclusions and possibilities. Lateral thinking is closely associated with right brain hemispheric functioning.

Critical Thinking

Historically, critical thinking has occupied an important place in Western thought. The approach is again the subject of much attention today because it supports the development of intellectual and social competency in the learner and enables the individual to arrive at well-founded answers. The logical reasoning of Socrates and Aristotle demonstrated the three principal elements of critical thinking described by Glaser (1985): an attitude of thoughtful consideration of problems and subjects in one's own experience; knowledge of logical inquiry; and skill in applying these methods.

Utilizing Thought Patterns

Understanding of these three forms of thinking can be helpful to us in recognizing the variations in thought observed during intercultural communication. For example, literate persons from cultures that rely heavily on the written or printed word for information and learning may exhibit linear patterns whether they read and write from the left to the right or the right to the left side of a page, or from the top to the bottom or the bottom to the top of a page. Lateral patterns of thought may frequently be seen in cultures that transmit information primarily through oral exchange or through visual representations that do not include words. Logical inquiry, which is so much a part of the critical thinking process, employs linear approaches. When persons from cultures with predominantly linear patterns encounter persons from cultures with predominantly lateral patterns, communication may be difficult without major adjustments. These adjustments are especially important in intercultural educational training, or learning settings.

The challenge for persons interested in improving their intercultural communication skills is to recognize their own thinking and learning styles or preferences, to determine the predominant styles and preferences of others from a different cultural background, and to establish a suitable communication match.

It is important to note here that the thinking patterns presented above represent only three of many other patterns that might be observed throughout the world. Differing patterns of thought may be reflected and observed in individual and group discussions and generally vary based on the discussion's timing, purpose, or focus; patterns may also vary in the use of the information generated, in the persons involved and types of involvement, and in the settings preferred. That is, as discussed earlier, persons in some cultures concentrate on reaching "the point" as soon as possible and others savor "round about" methods of reaching conclusions in a relaxed time frame. Some individuals or groups may seek to focus or to guide the thinking of others toward particular information, or toward the use of information, while others may encourage the generation of content from the group and active member involvement in the decision-making process.

Story telling may be preferable to fact-giving in many cultures. In others the highlighting or discovering of analogies is often the important goal rather than the reaching of final or set conclusions. In still other cultures the initiation of the direction of thought may often belong to one individual but the direction of discussion may be shared by all members.

Just as an understanding of thought patterns is an important area of skill development in intercultural communication, knowledge of right and left brain hemispheric preferences will be helpful to you in discovering similarities and differences among cultures. This information, like the content focused on learning in this chapter, is especially relevant for work, training, and learning settings.

RIGHT/LEFT BRAIN
HEMISPHERIC PREFERENCES

The work of Roger Sperry (1968) and Robert Ornstein (1972) resulted in our recent understanding of function of the brain. The two sides of the brain are seen to control opposite functions. The right, or "creative," side (related to lateral thought) processes functions related to color or imagination, for example; the left or "logical," side (related to linear thought) processes language or sequential and number-related functions. Although the two hemispheres share some of the processing and, having two sides of the brain, people use both, many persons evidence preferences for right or left mode approaches and these preferences are reflected in their thinking.

A knowledge of left and right hemispheric function is helpful to us because it enables us to recognize our own individual methods of processing and the patterns of processing preferred by others (de Bono, 1983). Although everyone has a brain with two sides, we do have options and we often make use of the opportunity to "lean" to the right or to the left in our thought processing. Our thinking styles may be just as reflective of our cultures, our values and our skills as our general behavior.

Evidence of our hemispheric preferences may be found in our favorite activities, our choices of subjects to study, and the work we perform. These preferences may be consciously or unconsciously directed but are most frequently reflected in our unconscious behavior. In other words, we are unaware that we are making a choice.

We can, however, learn (consciously) to direct our behavior toward either side of the brain and to shift from left to right at will. This ability is a valuable skill in the learning setting, for example, because some subjects require the use of a particular mode of processing more than others. When we choose a particular subject, we are probably selecting it because our thinking skills are most comfortably matched to the thinking skills appropriate for that area's functioning. The subject may be "easy" for us because our skills are matched to the processing function required. When we have difficulty in a particular subject area, it may be because we must "shift" our approach to match our thinking style to the necessary processing function and the approach leaves us feeling "stuck" in the process.

When classroom subjects are required courses, we must be able to shift our thinking to the side of the brain that can best accommodate the necessary thought processes. When we make discoveries on our own and get stuck, it is one thing; but finding ourselves stuck in an area of discovery against our will may cause real difficulty for us. For example, liking to read, we might decide to pursue an area of interest at the library only to find some of the information beyond our grasp. We have, however, the option of re-directing our learning experience. We have initiated and structured the experience so we can design another experience of our choice. On the other hand, liking to read but finding ourselves in a required laboratory course, with little reading material and ability, we may have little or no opportunity to substitute another experience. We may believe alternatives are not open to us. If our hemispheric preference is "left" and the subject demands skills related to the "right," we have a problem-solving situation. What to do? Where to go? How to cope? The predicament can be especially trying or frustrating if we (or our instructors) are unaware of the causes of the difficulty. The problem is ours and must be solved by ourselves in these situations.

If we (or our instructors), are aware of the causes of the problem, we can learn to shift in order to use our preferred hemisphere in another way to accomplish the task at hand. If this is not the case, we may be forced to struggle and our attitudes may shoot forth to advise us that "this is not the subject for us!" Few of us **like** to be frustrated or to fail, especially if our culture views failure as the end of it all, to be avoided at all costs. Often, the learning or discoveries inherent in most failure may not be observable.

Recognition of our own hemispheric preferences and the related skills of that hemisphere can help us achieve success because our **strengths** will be exposed; but recognition of preferences which require shifts from one hemisphere to the other can help us use both sides of the brain more effectively.

In our general culture, approaches and materials are usually designed for left hemispheric function. The linear arrangements of materials, the formats and approaches to instruction, do not usually present the need for extensive right hemispheric functioning. Reading, writing, and mathematics all require the use of left brain processes and the daily use of these subjects encourages us to develop left brain skills in order to learn.

One of the reasons for this linear orientation is that our learning settings, from the earliest years, are designed for group learning with the direction resting in the hands of the teacher. With this new understanding of brain functioning, new approaches and materials must be designed for group use and for group centered direction. It isn't so much that schools are not directing their attention toward the individuals involved, but more the realization that the work must be accomplished—teachers and students together—within a given timeframe over a given period during the week or month or years; this is necessary in order to recognize the learning that has taken place. The resource material provided is then sequenced so that learners focus on particular content at a particular time in a particular order.

It is not even so much that this approach can't be accommodated by most of the learners, but that the right hemispheric processing functions are put on hold while the left gears are engaged to move us along. The approach works fine for most of us, but not as well as it might. That may be because some subjects require right processing and even these may be taught and structured for left processing (Edwards, 1986).

What often happens is that, somewhere along the line, some of us "tune out" and screen our inability to acquire needed skills in a particular subject because we can't get into left gear. That is, we often move (physically or mentally) to search for other approaches to learning that might work for us.

These alternate avenues are usually selected because they match our interests and they are tried on to see if they match our skills. As mentioned earlier, the choices may or may not match our skills in the end, but at least we select them. We are free to approach learning in our way. These approaches usually engage us actively in the use of both sides of the brain—left and right—using linear and lateral thinking patterns. For this reason, self-directed learning approaches—the approaches to learning that most adults use in daily life—accommodate the needs of the adult learner effectively both in and outside of formal learning settings (Knowles, 1975). The teacher or the learner in any setting, including the intercultural program must keep this concept in mind in order to most effectively communicate meaning: all students must be allowed—or must find a way—to approach learning in the way most effective for them.

Learners do not, however, always recognize that learning occurs all around them in everyday settings, or that learning is a process that occurs through a mixture of left and right brain functioning, or that this functioning may be directed by themselves. But learners who do recognize the relationship between these factors and their success in learning may recognize the need to transfer the skills used in everyday learning to more formal or structured settings. That means knowing when and where to use linear or lateral thinking patterns and knowing when and where to employ left and right brain processing or combinations of both. Our brain does the job for us if we put it in gear.

For example, think of writing a letter. How do you begin?

Do you make an outline? Most of us work in a linear format with a series of sentences within a date, salutation, and signature. As the "pictures" form in our minds, we transfer our pictures to paper or to the computer or to a typewritten page. We usually concentrate on one or more of the pictures, pausing just long enough to "paint" our laterally processed picture in the linear framework that is provided. Does the letter make sense? Probably. Does it take concentrated thought? It may or may not, depending on the subject. Chances are, the process is not discomforting, but pleasurable, and words are not scratched out over and again or sheets of paper torn up. Words usually flow easily, or even quickly. Before we realize it, the letter is sealed. Even long letters are usually processed in this manner, allowing the brain to shift its functioning from right to left or left to right so that we see pictures. Seeing the pictures, we transfer them to the symbols that become "word pictures." The words and the pictures are our own; the framework and symbols have meaning for us and others, and most of the time we convey meaning in this manner fairly well.

The process may appear uncomplicated because we use our own pictures and our own words. In taking notes, for example, the framework is linear but our lateral processing can occur. We are able to sort and sift, to note "wholes" and "parts" of the message conveyed, and to transfer meaning in our own words. We may be limited by the degree to which we are familiar with the words conveyed but we will be able to see our word picture on the page. If we are taking notes in a lecture, the lecture is usually in a linear format and delivered in a compartmentalized fashion so the process is similar to the process with which we wrote our letter. We are given a "picture" by the lecturer, receive the words, translate them into a "mind picture," and paint our own "word picture" within a linear format.

The process may often be more difficult, however, when we, as teachers of multicultural learners, decide to deliver a lecture. How do we usually begin? By creating an outline, of course. Why? Because we have been taught to develop an outline and that lectures should be outlined so that the information is easily transferred by the lecturer and understood by the group.

The transfer of coherent information is one concern, but

the development of an outline is another. What is really our need? Our need is to creatively present a body of thoughts in a coherent fashion, two functions that require the processing by both hemispheres. To creatively identify the elements of the presentation, we need to "see" as many pictures as possible in order to sort; then we need to sort those to be presented.

When information is outlined using left brain functions and linear thinking, we begin by identifying topics, separating them into a logical order, and developing related subtopics under each. A perfectly logical process, it works and our brain can handle it.

If you would like to try another way, begin by identifying the topic you will address, and write the name of the topic on a piece of paper. Without evaluating whether or not to include it, think of everything that you know that is directly related to the topic that absolutely **must** (in your opinion) be included. Write one or a few descriptive words on the sheet, quickly connecting them to the topic.

For example, if your topic is driving responsibilities in a new culture, your first "picture" with its extended ideas might look something like that shown in Figure 6.1.

Do not erase or evaluate your picture, just continue to add descriptive words related directly to the topic or to the extensions as the words enter your mind. Your picture might now look something like that depicted in Figure 6.2.

Continue adding areas until you have created a "brain" or "mind" map that matches your needs for ideas for the lecture. When satisfied that you have enough areas represented, sort those of related interest that you will include with the lecture.

In this illustration, the result might resemble that shown in Figure 6.3.

You will discover that by using this method you will be able to identify areas of related interest in a shorter period of time than by using the traditional method of outlining. You are able to do this because you are able to transfer "thought pictures" as quickly as you can write (or more quickly), if you don't have to organize and evaluate **first**.

If you use the traditional method, you have the pictures in your mind but you can't "see" all of them as rapidly as they

Figure 6.1 Mind Map Development, Phase 1

Figure 6.2 Mind Map Development, Phase 2

appear, so you pause to think about what should or should not be transferred to the paper. By transferring **first**, you are able to list quickly, to easily sort the areas you wish to develop, and to then place your picture in a linear or left brain framework for development.

Buzan (1983, p. 102) has described the difficulties faced by a 14-year-old boy who could not complete a **written** outline easily but could easily and quickly organize his thinking with a brain map.

Another way of observing the lateral/right brain fashion in

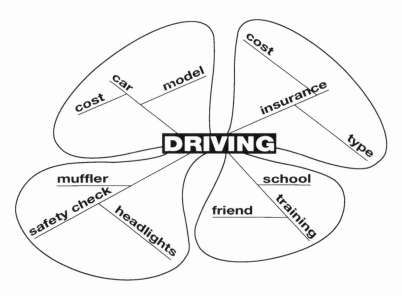

Figure 6.3 Mind Map Development, Phase 3

which the brain works is to map the conversation of a young child with a fairly limited vocabulary who is beginning to speak but is not yet writing. As the patterns of thought are conveyed, you will see the variety of associations (accompanied by body motions and gestures that convey meaning when we don't have the words). The example (see Figure 6.4) was mapped when listening to the conversation of a three-year-old girl.

Children also exhibit the ability to shift easily between the left and right hemispheres and these shifts can be readily observed in children who have begun to speak and to converse but are not yet able to read or to write. The following pattern was observed in a five-year-old girl (see Figure 6.5).

One of the reasons lateral function is readily observed in young children is that linear or left hemisphere patterning has not yet become a daily habit. As reading, writing, and math or other left hemisphere related subjects become a part of the daily curriculum, the related skills tend to encourage the "leaning" to the left mentioned earlier. Figure 6.6 presents a summary

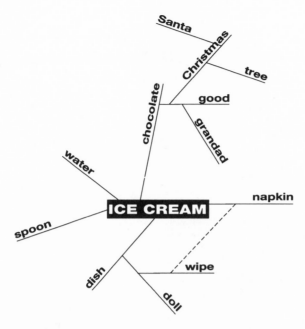

Figure 6.4 Patterns of Thought—3-Year-Old Girl

of the comparisons of left/right hemispheric functions noted by Edwards (1979, p. 40).

An area of skill building that might be helpful to you is the determination of your own hemispheric and linear/lateral preferences. This self-discovery can occur informally by looking at your present preferences: hobbies, work, recreation, learning areas (formal and informal classes, seminars, etc.), and learning styles (how **you** learn best). Relate your activities to the right or left hemisphere functions described by Edwards. It is important to remember that shifts are occurring between the areas of the brain anyway, even as an activity requires more functioning in one particular hemisphere than in the other. If you understand your own learning preferences, you will likely be more alert to the learning needs of your multicultural friends or students.

Recent studies of the brain and its functions indicate that high levels of logic and problem-solving ability appear to be

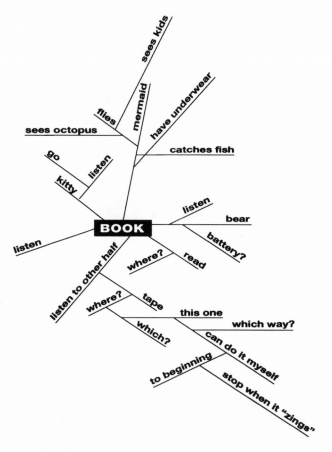

Figure 6.5 Patterns of Thought—5-Year-Old Girl

related to the simultaneous use of both hemispheres, a process called lateralization. Approaches to training and learning or work that encourage "whole brain thinking" are to be supported in skill development that is directed toward the improvement of intercultural communication.

As a student of intercultural communication—or as a teacher—you can aim to learn or to teach by utilizing the whole brain. Indications are that we have capabilities beyond our imaginations! More research is necessary but as Samples (1977, p.

Left-Mode	Right-Mode
1. Verbal: words; descriptions; definitions	1. Nonverbal: things, less connection to words
2. Analytic: part-by-part; step-by-step	2. Synthetic: "wholes"; putting together
3. Symbolic: something standing for something	3. Concrete: as it is at the moment
4. Abstract: a bit represents the whole	4. Analogic: metaphoric relationships; seeing likenesses
5. Temporal: first things first, second things second; sequenced	5. Nontemporal: without sense of time
6. Rational: reason; facts leading to conclusions	6. Nonrational: not requiring facts; willing to suspend judgment
7. Digital: numbers; counting	7. Spatial: relationships; how parts form wholes
8. Logical: relating one thing to another to draw conclusions	8. Intuitive: hunches, feelings, visual images; leaps of insight
9. Linear: linked ideas; one thought following another directly leading to a convergent conclusion	9. Holistic: seeing wholes at once; perceiving patterns and structure; leading to divergent conclusions

Figure 6.6 Left-Mode and Right-Mode Characteristics of Human Brain Functioning

688) has observed: "Recent research has dispelled the notion that humans possess five senses. Even the tokenism that acknowledges the 'sixth sense' is absurd . . . (because) awareness sensors in us may number well above 20." It is important to provide yourself or your students with opportunities to learn through as many of those awareness sensors possible.

LEARNING NEEDS AND STYLES

Although this book is designed for use by persons in a variety of roles, this chapter has been said to relate especially to the needs of those in work, training, or learning settings. The learning needs and styles of learners may be as varied as the individuals themselves, although particular group patterns and preferences may be seen within and across cultures. For this reason, a review of particular learning needs and styles is helpful in preparing for successful intercultural communication and interaction.

Learning is Personal

Learners must be able to recognize their own needs so that learning is seen as a personal responsibility to be directed by themselves, even when structures and formats are designed by others. Adult learners should become increasingly aware of their own need to relate their lateral or linear patterns and preferences to existing programs, activities, or opportunities. It is possible for learners with either preference to function more effectively if they are able to direct their strengths toward the subjects at hand and to find ways of their own to meet learning needs.

When structures or formats are directed toward the use of particular patterns, learners must be aware of the alternatives open to them for using patterns more compatible with their learning styles. For example, the use of a brain or mind map approach to outlining may also be useful in accomplishing other assignments in formal or informal settings. It is important to help learners to develop self-directed learning styles. Self-directed learners who are aware of their capabilities as self-directed learners are then able to learn in structures with formats determined by others, as well as to create structures and formats for themselves. Structure may become less of a concern than who creates it and how we work within it.

It is important to enable learners to direct their learning in intercultural settings because the learner has more freedom to rely on personal strengths and resources. The matching of approaches to the learning styles and needs of the learners reduces the possibility of cultural bias in the selection of methods and resources that might conflict with local cultural values and customs.

Although supported internationally in theory and practice by adult educators and learners, self-directed learning may not be the approach of choice in certain instances. For example, in cultures where respect for the teacher (or trainer or instructor) and the teacher's knowledge is given first consideration, learner-initiated approaches would be considered discourteous.

Similar conclusions might be reached regarding the employment of traditional teacher-centered approaches with learners who are highly self-directed. The essential challenge for trainers or facilitators and learners is to determine and to meet learning needs—whatever the personal or cultural backgrounds of those involved.

Learning Needs

From the relationships presented in this chapter, you have seen that the processing of thought is not only complex but worthy of consideration in the development of skills related to intercultural communication and interaction.

We have not focused on the recognition of inability to process effectively for reasons related to physical, mental, or emotional factors. Impairments related to these areas of concern may affect thought processing, however, and may be observed in interaction across cultures. Cultures may vary in their general response to the needs of those who are unable to process information adequately and values related to this area of interaction will be reflected.

Responses to the learning needs of persons with hearing impairments, for example, may vary considerably with or without evidence of mental impairment. Sign language may or may not be taught in classes, for example, and in some areas has been forbidden. Teachers with hearing impairments may or may not be employed. Walker (1986) has described the impact of this "culture" (of the hearing impaired) on her family: the language, customs, and practices developed to support family members; the involuntary alienation or separation of family members from the larger society; the responses of persons without hearing impairments; and the general lack of understanding within the community. Each culture will have its own way of dealing with physical and mental learning needs.

Learning needs are the first consideration in relating approaches to skill development. The ability to identify personal needs has been cited as a necessary skill, one that can be shared with others in an intercultural environment at home or abroad. The information presented in this chapter is intended to help you apply information from a number of fields in a practical way to meet your own particular needs and to understand the needs of others.

Understanding the needs of others may require patience, sensitivity, the ability to compare and contrast patterns, or the ability to alter approaches and favorite practices in order to be effective. Understanding the needs of others may require you to practice receiving pictures rather than providing them, to recognize the difference between the creation of pictures transmitted through art and those transmitted through words, and to recognize the limitations of interpretation. You may find it difficult to see or to read another's "pictures"—to really understand—but results of an attempt to "see" may be worth the effort. The values are there.

Learning Styles

The ability to recognize in intercultural students appropriate learning styles and their relationship to the thinking process is an important skill. Kolb's Model is presented here in Figure 6.7 as an important resource for understanding thought processing experientially and for use with learners who prefer or might benefit from experiential approaches. Introduced by David Kolb (1976), the model serves as the basis for many current programs

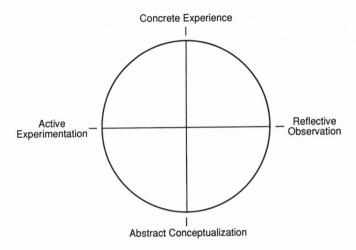

Figure 6.7 Kolb's Model

for adult learners that document and appropriately credit learning acquired through experience rather than traditional educational systems.

Because experiential learning moves from an experience to an understanding of the experience, the exercise below (which begins with an experience) might help you follow the stages illustrated in the model. You will need to make the distinction between learning and activities, that is, to recognize that learning may or may not have taken place during an activity. (Think of the classes or situations that you have been involved in where you might have learned and didn't!) You will need to focus your attention on what you understand and can do or feel differently about now than you did before the experience. As you complete the exercise, you will probably discover that you not only engaged in the experience, but have some assumptions about it to share, some theories of your own.

Exercise:

1. Think of a recent learning experience, something you learned by yourself or with others that was not credited as an academic course but is valuable to you.

2. With your *learning* in mind, complete the following:

    I learned how to. . . . .

    by. . . . .

    What actually happened?

    What observations did you make about the experience?

    What conclusions did you reach?

    How did you use this learning?

    How might you use this learning in the future?

    What would you do differently?

    Why?

3. How do your responses relate to the stages presented in Kolb's Model (See Figure 6.7)?

4. Do you recognize the stages that required more thinking than doing on your part? More doing than thinking?

Schools have traditionally presented information with a linear focus for the left brain. One reason for this is that the energies of teachers often flow easily when their own learning and teaching styles are matched. That is, teachers may prefer to approach the needs of learners using their own preferred modes. If this tendency is to be minimized, it is not only necessary for learners to identify their own learning styles—to be aware of their preferences—but to recognize the learning styles of others. Recognition of style differences and similarities in a group may make **all** the difference in your own learning or that of others during intercultural interaction.

Much research has been focused on learning styles in a variety of areas. Some researchers concentrated on the senses, citing the importance of sight, touch, taste, aural, and oral preferences. Others emphasized the relationship of the learner to the environment and variation in response to particular resources. Still others looked at cognition, perception and brain hemispheric processing. For example, Witkin (1974) studied preferences for working alone or with a group, independent-dependent "field" choices that extended to the choice of careers. Like Kolb, Gregorc (1977) and Renzulli and Smith (1978) developed inventories based on their respective research related to perceptual differences and instructional management learning styles. The research of Dunn and Dunn (1978) presented 18 elements that comprised learning style and emphasized the creation of an appropriate learning climate. McCarthy (1981) developed a model that linked four major styles and brain mode processing techniques.

For our purposes, you will need to reflect on your own style—how you learn best—and relate that information to the styles of others around you. It will help you to read about some of the work done by researchers mentioned above and to observe closely the individual and group variations among people of different cultural backgrounds. The knowledge gained from your observations will help you present information to people in a way that they understand (and thus appreciate) best.

Approaches to Learning

An understanding of the relationship between thought patterns, brain hemispheric preferences, learning needs or styles, and the major approaches to learning can be helpful when you select a learning setting or must determine your response within a particular setting. To help you narrow a great number of approaches to a workable few for observation or experience, four approaches will be reviewed here: experiential and theoretical; self-directed and other-directed. These approaches may be observed both within and outside of the United States. Because all of us are learners during intercultural interaction and exchange, knowing the differences in these approaches helps us recognize the similarities and differences in cultural response patterns. Knowing the differences helps us adjust our approaches to better meet our own needs and the needs of others.

Experiential

Experiential learning might be described as learning by doing. This approach enables the learner to move from the particular to the general; from the part to the whole. This approach is based on the assumption that people not only learn by doing, but they learn **best** by doing; the experience can be observed, conclusions may be reached through these observations, and the results can be evaluated to guide us toward new related experiences.

For example, imagine yourself in a rodeo stall on a bucking bronc when the chute is opened and you suddenly (very suddenly) enter the arena. What happens next? How do **you** feel about the experience? Why? What will you do as a result of this experience? Be honest!

If you are not an experienced rodeo participant or a rider par excellence, your answers might be similar to these:

1. I landed on the ground—and hard!

2. Sore! Afraid to get up. I wanted **out**! Anywhere! I thought I'd die! I thought I'd lost my senses!

3. Because I landed on my head. I realized the animal **had** the scene. I **knew** I'd lost my senses!

4. I'll see a doctor—a psychiatrist. I'll stay off bucking broncs or learn to ride better. I'll stick my head in a bucket of cool, cool water.

You have probably recognized the above example as a learning experience illustrating the stages of Kolb's Model which was introduced earlier. The model helps us see the thought processing necessary at all major levels of learning: cognitive, affective and performance; thinking, feeling, and doing. The Reflective Observation and Abstract Conceptualization levels illustrate the emphasis on thinking; the Concrete Experience and Active Experimentation phases emphasize performance. (Is feeling found throughout?) Both lateral and linear thought processing are required at all stages of movement in experiential learning. For this reason, use of experiential approaches in general, and the use of Kolb's Model as a resource in particular, are valuable tools for use by persons in intercultural settings.

Kolb's Learning Style inventory (1976) was normed in 1933 for adults 18 to 60 years of age. Two-thirds of the group were men; two-thirds had college degrees and represented diverse occupations and educational backgrounds. The group was fairly representative of many business or other career-focused settings and the inventory is often used in these settings to identify learning styles. If people are in work groups or teams in these settings, the results frequently show the variations in approaches to learning. The inventory measures how *you* see yourself, the kinds of problems you solve best and how you make decisions on the job. This kind of self-analysis is enlightening to learners of all kinds.

Kolb's theory is frequently applied to the process of portfolio development in the assessment of prior learning, or learning that has been acquired through life experiences. Competencies are identified in these experiences and matched with competencies expected of learners in programs based on credit (for example, in programs offering certification in a particular content area or in colleges and universities offering degrees). The Council for Adult and Experiential Learning (CAEL) is recognized nationally and internationally as the organization dedicated to supporting the validity of experiential learning and the reliable assessment of its outcomes. Because of its emphasis on learning through experience, Kolb's theory is especially effective with students who must overcome language barriers.

Kolb's Model and the assessment of prior learning process can be useful in the development of intercultural learning skills for several reasons. First, these resources are "transportable"; that is, they are generally adaptable across cultures. Secondly, these tools identify the *strengths* of the persons involved in relation to their work, training, or learning settings. Competency-focused, the assessment process highlights what the person knows and can do and documentation can be achieved using the person's own language.

Effective intercultural communication implies "connection"

through verbal and nonverbal exchange and interaction but your ongoing skill development depends on your ability to access and to use resources wisely. The resources presented in this chapter, as in other chapters, should be evaluated carefully as possible components of your framework for action and use across cultures.

Theoretical

Non-experiential (or theoretical) learning might be seen as learning by knowing. Non-experiential learning moves from the particular to the general, or from parts to wholes. Learners receive information that has been processed by others, reach conclusions, and may apply the learning later. It is the approach most frequently used in traditional classroom settings. In recent years, many of these settings have modified their approaches to include the assessment of prior learning, self-directed learning, or internships and practicums. These approaches have been introduced in university programs at undergraduate and graduate levels, in competency-based programs outside formal learning settings, and in some high schools.

Theoretical learning approaches are particularly suited to learners who process linearly using (primarily) the left side of the brain. Here the "picture" is presented to the learner to interpret and the interpretation is frequently "pictured" in written format or through discussion of inferences. A helpful comparison of experiential and non-experiential learning has been offered by Coleman (1977) which illustrates the similarities and differences as illustrated in Figure 6.8.

Self-Directed

Self-directed learning approaches are particularly noted among adult learners. These approaches are employed by adults in day-to-day informal learning settings in a variety of activities and in formal settings, as well (Tough, 1971). Programs structured to accommodate the needs of adult learners across cultures

Experiential Learning	Non-Experiential Learning
Particular to General	General to Particular
1. Carry out action; note effects	1. Receive information
2. Understand effects in terms of anticipating consequences if the same set of circumstances reoccurs	2. Assimilate; organize
3. Understand the general principle under which the instance falls; see the connection between the action and a range of circumstances	3. Infer; relate
4. Apply through action in a new circumstance within the range of generalization	4. Move from the cognitive and symbol processing sphere to the action sphere; apply

Figure 6.8 A Comparison of Experiential and Non-Experiential Learning

consider the adult's preference for problem-related activities which offer opportunities for direct application of the skills acquired.

Thinking patterns employed in the formal classroom may vary from those employed by the adult in daily activities. In the performance of these activities, the adult is able to move freely between linear and lateral approaches when learning or solving problems. The learning is carried out without the limitations often encountered in formal settings. The needs of adult learners from all cultures must be recognized and effectively addressed if success is to be achieved in formal and informal structures.

Self-directed approaches increase the chances that the learner may move freely between the use of linear and lateral approaches because the learner experiences more freedom in the selection of the content which is to be learned; the learner is free to set personal goals, to identify and select resources and related activities, and to evaluate the results of learning. When all, or the majority, of these functions are defined by others, attention must be given to the skills that are necessary for learner success in relating to these various aspects of the program. The degree to which learners are enabled to use either or both sides of the brain as desired is a particular consideration in formal settings.

Other-Directed Learning

The chances of learning success are directly related to the degree to which a learner is able to use personal strengths in processing information. In formal settings, the design of programs allowing for these individual differences is usually the responsibility of others and learning remains predominantly linear in structure and format. The skills necessary for success, therefore, are usually oriented toward left-brain functioning and linear processing. The important consideration may be only a question of how far those responsible for program design, development, and implementation are willing to go to provide a setting meeting the needs of all learners.

RELATING CONCEPTS TO SKILL BUILDING

The content of this chapter was designed to help you move from a theoretical or knowledge base to understanding and to practice levels, to help you relate your understanding to communication and interaction in an intercultural setting.

For this reason, you may wish to do some personal brainstorming at this time regarding a particular culture and the observations or comparisons you might wish to make regarding (a) thought patterns, (b) learning styles, and (c) approaches to learning.

With your ideas in mind, attention should be given to the intercultural and personal considerations addressed below.

Intercultural Considerations

Conversation and discussion

Conversation and discussion may be major parts of intercultural interaction if language is not a barrier. But language is not the only barrier to communication. Thought patterns and other factors often interfere. For example, linear patterns may conflict with lateral patterns, particularly when the persons involved are from highly verbal cultures.

Suggested Experience:

1. Participate in discussions or conversations of varying length with several persons from **your own** culture who have learning patterns *opposite* your own.

2. What was your maximum comfort level? (How long did you last?)

3. How did you react?

Conversation and discussion patterns in intercultural settings must be considered, but approaches to problem solving often become a concern as well, particularly in training settings. In addition, in these settings thought patterns may be influenced by other factors, such as time, that may be problematic.

Problem Solving and Training

The relationship of problem-solving approaches to intercultural communication and interaction is an important one and observation should be directed especially toward the typical cultural roles of individuals in relation to groups. Hall (1989) has described the similarities and differences between the way monochronic groups and cultures go about transacting business or problem solving and the manner in which polychronic cultures address the issue.

Polychronic approaches usually involve a number of people

doing a number of things at the same time. Monochronic approaches tend to focus on one-thing-at-a-time. In this approach the tendency is to tighten the time frame, using monochronic approaches so that one thing is accomplished quickly and before addressing other issues. The aim in polychronic approaches is to depend on information arriving from a number of directions which may or may not arrive at the same time, so time frames are flexible.

The differences between these approaches are evident when meetings are scheduled at a particular time and persons in the monochronic mode have to wait for those in a polychronic mode or when products or results are not evident within a particular time frame.

Although these patterns are related to the way people approach interaction more than to individual processing patterns, the approach may influence problem solving through the attitudes of those involved. When monochronic modes do not enable persons to allocate adequate time for the lateral exchange of information, and when they present a linear format and approach, difficulties often appear. Polychronic approaches, on the other hand, may be limited in terms of effective results.

Polychronic approaches may cause frustration for those preferring monochronic approaches and their efficiency may be negatively affected. These situations must be recognized as conflicting patterns of approach to problem solving, rather than lack of the ability to solve problems effectively.

Following a one-thing-at-a-time linear format or a many-things-at-a-time lateral format can influence schedules, and schedules handled so differently may influence the amount of time allowed for problem solving, the time the person or culture requires for attaining the preferred results. Thought processing may then become related to time. When these time-related approaches differ, conflict may be noted, as in a description by Hall (1989, p. 230) in the *Dance of Life*, a study of the influence of time in the lives of individuals and cultures. For example, in cultures where it may be difficult to determine whether schedules exist or not, attempts to have set times for work, meetings, seminars and workshops, or classroom sessions may be difficult, if not impossible. You may then need to consider an alternate approach to your own use of time in this circumstance.

Suggested Experience:

1. In your own culture, practice *extending* and *reducing* the time it normally takes you to solve a problem of your choice, to run a meeting, or to present training.

2. How was your thinking affected?

Personal Considerations

With the information you have at this time, how would you describe the following:

1. Your thought pattern(s)?

2. Your learning style(s)?

3. The approaches you prefer in a learning setting?

4. Your learning needs at this time?

5. The resources (people, places, things) that might help you most?

6. The comparison of your framework for action at this time with the suggested framework?

SUMMARY

Thought patterns, brain hemispheric preferences, and individual similarities or differences have been the focus of this chapter, noting the importance of developing the ability to recognize these similarities and differences. Recognition of the values reflected in these often cultural patterns and preferences will be helpful to you in understanding other cultures during interaction and in your ongoing skill development.

CHAPTER 7

Speaking

The primary focus of this chapter is on verbal communication and the role of language in cultures. Primary considerations include speech patterns, the relation of speech to writing, and skill building.

Chapters 3 through 6 have emphasized the importance of valuing, observing, listening, and thinking in effective intercultural interaction. Because all of these skill areas are related to each other in interaction, it is well to note the "connectedness" of these skill areas to speaking, the fifth area of consideration for your action framework, and it is helpful to identify necessary speaking components.

SPEECH PATTERNS

Because of their influence on oral exchanges in interaction, two patterns of speech addressed in Chapter 5 should also be considered in this chapter: frequency and duration. These patterns vary among individuals and cultures and, in addition to individual styles and preferences, are readily observed.

Frequency and Duration

How often a person speaks (frequency) and how long a person continues to speak (duration) may be influenced by many factors. During the development of your intercultural communication skills, you will need to be aware of these particular factors in order to interact effectively and to understand the behavior of others. It is important to know not only **what** is occuring but **why**.

Influencing Factors

The limitations addressed regarding the linear arrangement of words may be an influencing factor during the verbal exchange of language. For example, the structure of the language or words may not convey messages adequately. In *The Hidden Culture*, Hall (1976, p. 49) described this problem. "The paradox of culture is that language, the system most frequently used to describe culture, is by nature poorly adapted to this difficult task. It is too linear, not comprehensive enough, too slow, too limited, too constrained, too unnatural, too much a product of its own evolution, and too artificial."

Is it possible that, for some persons, their thought patterns are such that they find use of the language burdensome—consciously or unconsciously? Other factors, too, may influence the process of speaking, a complex process using words to interpret thoughts and to place thoughts in the channels of others to be interpreted as we "think" them.

For example, the tendency to follow the cultural patterns of our particular groups or cultures is strong. Is it possible that persons in highly verbal cultures develop the habit because that is the way most people around them communicate? Is there another possible answer? It may be easier to follow an accepted pattern than to exercise individual preference, especially when local values may or may not accommodate deviations from established norms. A degree of risk may then be attached to the speaking process, risk that may actually render persons "speechless" under particular circumstances.

Under slightly different circumstances, it has been observed that persons may be rendered "speechless" when making "shifts" between the hemispheres of the brain. The person who, for example, engaged in a particular activity, may be observed to pause during the activity in order to speak. These persons may find it difficult, if not impossible, to engage in conversation and the particular activity at the same time. Persons around them may often view this "pattern" as unusual, especially if their own patterns are different.

So the contest between individuals begins. Shall we try to relate to their patterns or to my own? Shall we attempt to interfere with their processing or to encourage them to adjust it so we will understand? Shall we adjust the activity itself as we understand it so **they** can perform it as we understand it?

Words and Creativity

Words may, indeed, interfere with an individual's ability to engage in a creative activity and the reasons for this have been explained by Edwards (1979) in relation to art. For example, a person may find it impossible to draw and to speak at the same time. These persons may converse, pause in order to pursue the activity, and resume conversation when attention to the activity ceases. The processing of thought that is related to the activity must be interpreted throughout the activity, and other data related to speech and conversation must be delivered through the established method, the use of words. Words have configurations and meanings of their own. The configurations and meaning of words must not only be **shared** to be understood, but the ideas and relationships associated with the particular activity must be presented for another person to understand.

This exchange of words and ideas related to a creative activity may be difficult, especially if the person engaged in the activity tends to be more proficient at processing and presenting ideas visually. Creative people often "speak" best through presentation of their creative products. An individual's proficiency may be more difficult to demonstrate when attempting to convey meaning in two areas at the same time: the production of the product and the production of words.

It is important to note here that both the creative product and the words convey meaning. Each person has processed information and presented products to be mutually shared and understood. Both products might be misunderstood. Visual products, however, present the "whole" picture and the relationship of the parts can be seen. The products delivered verbally arrive in parts and the "whole" must be created by the receiver: a picture within the mind.

A visual product may elicit questions on the part of a receiver but the creator and the receiver are **seeing** the same product. Word products may require the creator and the receiver to continue questioning until both parties are convinced they "see" the same picture, that they understand. For this reason, discussions of printed information may require longer periods of time to reach understanding than discussion regarding a visible product.

Words and Understanding

The heavy reliance on the use of printed material in traditional learning settings **requires** learner's discussion for understanding. The need to discuss is frequently expressed by adult intercultural learners and others who must process a great deal of printed material. For this reason, discussion should be included in programs for adults which rely not only on the printed but the spoken word and include a great deal of lecturing.

Is it any wonder that the products of an artist may not be understood by others or that our own personal or cultural patterns of delivering words may be misunderstood? Language and verbal exchanges may be difficult to fully comprehend because the "pictures" of the mind must be "illustrated" through words rather than as pictures.

Is it any wonder that a lateral process, restricted to linear presentation (the left side of the brain) becomes difficult to understand? The dimensions of this restriction have been described by Edwards (1979) as affecting the ability of an individual to demonstrate a lateral function (art) through instructions delivered in linear fashion (words). The person's own pictures must be interpreted in terms of the arrangement and the meanings of the words presented (another picture). The person often finds it difficult to sort through the resulting maze to locate the reservoir of innate ability that is naturally present. The search for ways to cope may be difficult for the individual and for those who want to help without a knowledge of these processing differences. Telling someone what to do does not mean the person will be able to do it; in fact, it may decrease the chances of successful application of the information under certain circumstances.

Processing and Involvement

The degree to which individuals and groups rely on the processing and presentation of information in linear or lateral formats may be reflected in the nonverbal as well as the verbal presentations observed. Art and other creative products "speak" in a language all their own and it is helpful to practice learning this language.

In studies of cultures with high verbal involvement styles, Tannen (1990) notes that persons with these verbal patterns may be perceived as interrupting the conversations of speakers from other areas. Where patterns of involvement varied in marked degree, those with high involvement styles were frequently considered rude. Tannen observed, however, that these same persons might be considered polite at home or in their local areas.

Is it possible that persons perceived as delaying the movement of communication in one area may be perceived in their own areas as highly verbal? That persons considered highly verbal in a particular area are perceived as delaying the movement of conversation in their own areas of residence?

These and other questions must receive attention when observing or listening and speaking in our own and in other cultures. The question of who dominates whom verbally may be more related to preferred patterns of communication than to inclinations on the part of an individual or group of individuals to dominate verbally. The real question lies in our individual and group responses to differences in patterns of communication. We must decide and we must respond. Shall we rely on our own approaches? Attempt to alter the approaches of others? Alter our own approaches? Scream?

The choice is **really** ours.

The Influence of Voice

Recognizing Voice Quality

One aspect of speech that may influence group movement is the quality of the voices present during interaction. All of us have known persons with voices that seemed to "get on our nerves" or to "drive us to distraction." It wasn't so much the conversations with these people but the sound of the voices that (literally) distracted us. If the conversations or discussions were lengthy, we might have considered one or more of the choices we presented earlier in response to difficult situations. If the conversations were short, we might have heaved great sighs of relief.

Tone quality can be a problem for us, especially if (you guessed it) the quality is not like that to which we are accustomed. In day-to-day interaction within a culture or in interaction with friends in our local areas, it may be easy to forget that most cultures not only have language differences but exhibit qualities in the speech patterns that are attached to each language. The ups and downs, the elevations and plunges or swoops and swishes can create a sound all their own. Sounds released when a conversation begins may move a group and its members forward or backward and all places in between. A word aims for the ceiling and bounces back with a thud. Language sounds may move around us like the regulated beats of a chorus line on stage.

Recognizing Sounds

Some language sounds are like the sound of birds or gurgling brooks. Others may fall on our ears like raindrops on the rooftops or tinkling bells. The variations of sound in language and words may appear endless and this is an aspect of language that is observable. Recognition of these sounds is a special area of study related to your skill development that can be approached informally through practice.

Languages are often taught through music, particularly through individual and group singing. Music facilitates the learning process by linking words to rhythmic patterns and levels and sound—in sync time. These relationships can be experienced by trying to learn an unfamiliar poem with and without music. The **feeling** of lateral thought processing is present, even as the linear framework improves restrictions of time and lyrics.

Observing sound mixtures and levels associated with language can be helpful to you in discovering patterns, individual and group similarities, and differences. You will probably improve your listening skills, recognize the relationship between group movement, and view the language in a new way.

Informal and Formal

Another observable that can be easily discovered is the relationship between formal and informal uses of language in the environment around us. Most cultures reserve particular kinds of communication patterns for their own use in private, at home settings and other patterns for use in public. The ease with which people exchange information and interact among family members and close friends is recognized by most of us, and the fact that behavior may change with others outside the familiar network is recognized widely.

Informal

One reason for this behavioral division between language forms is that people may feel accepted at home, with close friends and family, where the patterns of interaction are known. Where patterns of interaction are unknown, the question of ability to interact successfully may arise. This "fear of the unknown," however slight, may be especially present, for example, when learning a language. Let's face it. Who wants to demonstrate vulnerability in public? The folks at home are accustomed to seeing our mistakes. It's "*ok*" to share a lack of knowledge or skills with them because we are aware of their own inadequacies. We're on safe ground. "I might not know the language, but you don't know it either so we're equal, aren't we?" Relaxed informal language mirrors the more relaxed feelings most people relate to the safety of "home."

Facing the unknown, however, is different. We know our capabilities and some of our limitations, but we're never quite sure what's "out there" that might mean facing another challenge or risk—and we have enough, don't we?

The language used at home may be similar to or different from the language spoken in the local area. Individual and group variations may be present to larger or smaller degrees, but the informal language of a culture may be readily observed and, if not shared, recognized by members within the culture. The act of "putting it into my own words" may mean putting it into the words representative of commonly shared values and preferences with the particular culture. The use of private language conveys a feeling of "belonging"—to a family, a group, a race, or a culture. Language was invented to be shared.

Formal

The risks attached to sharing ourselves, our ideas, our words with the public, however, are greater. When we use the expression "I just want to let down my hair," it frequently means we're going home or to be with friends or family where we can be more comfortable. The expression implies we do something else with our hair in public. Do we use the expression "I put on my best face" when speaking of relationships with family? These expressions reflect our closeness and our feelings of security or love with our "private ones" and the added stress felt when we are in public situations.

Public

Verbal interaction with the public may differ from that observed in private settings in a variety of areas: work and activity related experiences, or learning and professional areas, for example. Each of these areas, and others related to daily interaction, may have a "language" of its own. Words that pertain to a particular field, for example, may be known and understood by few people outside of the field or profession. Most professions create a language related to the profession that distinguishes the profession from others. Just as the private language of an individual or group is reserved for special use of the individual or group, the public language is reserved for the group, as well.

Special Language and Groups

These uses of special languages within special groups can be observed in conversations with members of most professions, in schools and hospitals, in corporations and churches. Frequently, the language may be so unintelligible to persons outside of the "culture" that conversations may be brief or difficult and exchanges between and across "cultures" may be infrequent or they may not occur at all. In fact, some of these "cultural" language variations may be more difficult to acquire than the readily recognized languages of the culture.

Special Language and Position

The diversity of languages within a particular culture may not only be recognized in terms of private or public usage focused on work, career, or community groups, but also in terms of the language used to define status, rank, or position. This language is recognized in the use of titles assigned to royalty; to older persons; to persons attaining particular degrees, diplomas or certificates; or to persons in the military or in other forms of service.

In most cases, special forms of address or expressions of courtesy or recognition are used in the company of the person.

The forms of language associated with status may be spoken only by the members of a particular group, or formal usage may be expected in the presence of these persons. In some cultures, special forms of the language are reserved for particular rituals and events or ceremonies. These forms of the language are frequently observed in religious ceremonies and events where the language may be "sung" by the leader through elevations of the voice while speaking or reading a prayer.

One-to-One

Culturally significant similarities and differences in speech and conversational patterns may be observed when two persons engage in conversation. These patterns may be particularly apparent in exchanges between youth and adults, persons with different status designations, older and younger persons, or persons of different sexes.

Conversational patterns between youth and adults may be seen to vary from flexible and open to highly structured exchanges. Youth, for example, may exhibit formal courtesies in the presence of adults that would not be exhibited with other young people within the culture. Handshakes, curtsies, or other forms of respect may accompany the verbal exchanges. Greetings and departures may be signaled by the removal of a hat or other symbolic gestures of respect. Special salutations or farewells may be regularly observed as part of the daily practices within the culture.

In particular cultures, verbal exchanges between youth and adults may be frequent and informal with little or no distinction or difference in terms of the language expressed. In other cultures, observable differences are evident in the cultural patterns of exchanges between youth and adults and between youth and youth.

These cultures may often expect behavior from children who are in the presence of adults to differ from that reserved for the children's peers. Because cultures vary considerably regarding who may be designated an adult, determining appropriate intercultural exchanges may be difficult. For example, youth-oriented cultures may avoid marked distinctions in behavior between people according to age and few distinctions may be observable between youth and adults. Adult-oriented cultures may encourage marked distinctions in patterns of expression and the distinctions may appear more formal. These distinctions may apply to youth-adult relationships at home or simply in the external environment. Although the courtesies or exchanges of respect in the family vary from flexible to highly structured, most cultures have customary courtesies and expressions reserved for youth-adult interaction in the external or social environment.

Small and Large Groups

As noted in Chapter 5, when listening skills are highly developed it is often possible to discover the values of a people through close attention to their language and the related language patterns. The observation of small group verbal interaction is especially helpful in the identification of particular patterns or values because more people can become verbally involved in the exchanges of a small group. The larger the group, the fewer the chances of individual contributions to the total group. In the larger group each individual's contribution usually becomes centered on exchanges with another individual or a few individuals within the total group. For this reason, adult educators emphasize small group discussion and interaction in the learning setting and this approach is preferred by most adults. More people have an opportunity to speak.

If learners have received messages in centrally delivered presentations (in, for example, a university lecture), the need to exchange ideas regarding the topic usually surfaces. The need surfaces not only because learners must process the information in order to reach understanding, but because many learners learn best by processing ideas verbally through exchanges with others. This need is particularly evident in highly verbal populations where these exchanges with a small group may be initiated frequently and freely.

Often, people may be observed speaking at the same time (and understanding what is being said by the other speaker). If verbal activity is at a high level, one-to-one exchanges may be noticed in which one member almost completes the sentences of another, both nodding in agreement simultaneously and moving rapidly from one subject to another. Information may be exchanged in all directions at once, yet it appears to be understood and acknowledged by all members of the group.

This lateral exchange of information may not be preferred by persons from cultures evidencing a more focused (or linear) approach. Persons so inclined may reflect their preference by remaining attentive but quiet as they attempt to "see the train of thought" and to make sense of it all. For them, connections between the various aspects of the exchange must be processed in linear fashion.

Small Group Exchange

Small group exchanges offer persons involved the opportunity to question, to agree or disagree, and to reach personal, as well as group, conclusions. Small group exchanges also offer the person the opportunity to socialize or to affiliate, to feel a part of the larger environment, and to belong. Often conversation reflects this need as members of the group move to share needs or to support as necessary.

In a *Newsweek* article focused on the diverse uses of language in the United States, Kasindorf (1983, p. 49) described the "pidgin" spoken by so many surfers. Noting the special group focused design of the expressions, he observed: "Spending 15 minutes at Makaha Beach in Hawaii might make grown English teachers weep. But what those big classroom Kahunas— 'experts' in local lingo—don't grasp is that the local English is so bad it's **perfect.**"

The benefits of small group verbal exchanges are to be noted in peer counseling groups, therapy sessions, and small group problem-solving sessions. In every town or area, groups may be found exchanging ideas and determining solutions that could not be exchanged or determined in a large group.

Charles Kuralt (1985, p. 14) traveled all over the United States talking with people. "I have tried to go slow," he said, "stick to the backroads, take time to meet people, listen to yarns, notice the countryside go by, and feel the seasons change." He stopped on the road to talk with two men who had helped build the Golden Gate Bridge—fifty years ago.

> Kuralt: Can you believe that all that was fifty years ago?
> Zampa: No, just like yesterday. Just like yesterday. I got my fingerprints all over that iron, I'll tell you.
> Souza: Well, once in a while I come across the bridge and I look at those towers and look how high they are, yeah. And say, "I worked on that, I remember being up there." That's the feeling I get. It's a proud feeling. (p. 100)

The exchange of information described here could only have been shared by the persons involved and probably would not have been shared in the same way except through small group exchange.

To gain insight regarding any culture—national or other—it is well to reach as many people from as many groups as possible who are in as many roles as possible in order to discern major similarities and differences in oral exchange patterns. Since all members of a given population are rarely reached, even through our best efforts, we must usually settle for the information we are able to acquire, even though we must recognize its limitations.

Large Group Exchange

Large group exchanges are usually centralized, if the same messages are to be received by all. The reason is apparent. Each person cannot be heard by all (although the effort may be attempted in particular groups). For this reason, lecture may be selected as a method for ensuring consistent delivery of messages in crowded college or university classrooms, and the President of the United States delivers a televised "State of the Union" message. Leaders may be selected or elected within communities or groups or cultures to deliver a single message through their words, actions, and appearance. In some cultures, persons in positions of leadership simply impose their philosophies or messages on the people.

In these verbally centralized deliveries, the "train of thought" is discernible and the message usually proceeds without interruption. If opportunity for input is desired, questions are requested following the presentation of information. Under these circumstances, verbal opportunities for group thought processing are rare. Processing usually takes place in one-to-one or small group exchanges following the delivery.

It is important to note here that combinations of individual, one-to-one, and small and large group approaches are often observable. For example, leaders or representatives of large groups may actively seek input from their constituencies when preparing the messages for delivery or in problem-solving activities. The values of individuals and groups are reflected in these approaches and are observable.

Racial-Ethnic

Whether groups are large or small, the presence of racial-ethnic characteristics in speech patterns may be evident. People do not leave aspects of themselves behind when they enter a group but bring their values and preferences, their capabilities and roles with them. This means there may be observable speech patterns that are related to their racial-ethnic heritages. These patterns may often reflect variations in the languages that have evolved over the years, changing because of geographic relocations; Often the language may have altered in the presence of other language groups and patterns. In working toward improved intercultural communication be alert for language that mingles words from various languages; this might suggest that values and customs might have been assimilated from several cultures, as well.

Mobility and Attitudes

Mobile populations often select words from other groups and these words become part of their daily speech. These words may be altered to accommodate the needs of the particular culture or group. Shifting populations often retain, as well, aspects of their "home language" that may remain relatively unaltered and stable during the years of relocation. When this happens, the language spoken in the country or community (culture) of origin may change over a period of time, even as the original characteristics are retained among people who relocated.

Cultures are seen to vary in their willingness to acquire a new language, with some speaking several, or even many, languages and others speaking one or a few. The acquisition of language may be based on personal attitudes and preferences, but is influenced by other factors. These may include the nature of the geographical location, the cultural values of groups, and the degree of exposure to other languages. In some cases, people may be deprived of the opportunity to speak the language of their cultural heritage and required to acquire another or to rely on the acquisition of another for daily interaction.

Influence of Interaction

Multicultural populations that interact freely and speak several languages may also reflect the values of their racial-ethnic heritage through language. That is, particular expressions that are related to the racial-ethnic origins of a group may be observable and, in many cases, acquired by others. It is possible, in these situations, to observe persons of a particular race or ethnic group using words and expressions from another group in their private or public speech.

In some cultures, where there are many people of the same racial heritage, but with a variety of ethnic groups, the languages spoken by the various groups may be so varied that few groups may understand each other within the total culture. Verbal exchanges may be difficult. These groups may speak the languages of other racial or ethnic groups beyond their geographical area.

In other cultures, multicultural populations may interact freely but rely on a particular language within the total culture. In those areas, particular groups may speak the language related to their racial-ethnic heritage, or additional languages, as well as the predominant language of the culture.

Gender Related

In some cultures the influence of gender on the verbal exchanges between individuals has been recognized as an important factor. Studies have noted the differences, for example, between the way girls may converse and the way boys may converse. In the United States these patterns have been described by Tannen (1990) and by Gilligan (1982) with regard to the physical positions of girls speaking with girls and of boys speaking with boys. Topics and positions were different for each group. Boys were seen to be in parallel positions with each other, with less eye contact, and girls were seen to be facing each other with frequent eye contact. The conversations of girls were usually focused on personal or people-related concerns, of boys on activities or sports.

Studies related to the frequency and duration of speech have also been focused on adult males and females in small and large groups. These studies described men in groups as not only speaking more frequently than women but as interrupting more frequently.

These and other studies have related the differences in language patterns to differences observed in male and female children at play. The conclusions highlighted the two groups' opposite goals that appeared related to their approaches to play. Girls appeared focused on cooperative approaches and boys appeared focused on competitive approaches. These differences were reflected in the language patterns observed (Tannen, 1990).

Although the interaction of males and females varies widely

across cultures, the presence of males in positions of power encourages their use of public and formal language patterns, in addition to private exchange. In cultures where women share public roles with men, these public patterns are observed for both men and women. It is important to note that in countries where women remain uneducated or undereducated in relation to men, women may rely almost exclusively on the use of private patterns.

On the other hand, in cultures where literacy rates are low, men and women may not benefit from the opportunity to increase their ability to use more formal patterns of language and private approaches may prove inadequate for their needs.

Respect Related

In most cultures, concern for the feelings and customs of others is honored through the use of the language. Words that cause discomfort for others are readily identified and generally avoided.

Courtesy

A specific cultural "no-no" is determined by cultural values and the cultures concerned. This means that what may be considered discourteous in one culture may not be considered discourteous in another. A commonality, however, is the desire to render respect through the use of language, whatever form that takes.

Most cultures have a cultural "set" of obscenities, racial slurs, or epithets that may emerge when tempers are short or prejudice is present or devaluation of the status of another individual or group is attempted through the use of words. Understanding which words these are, and why they are used, will help you as you respond to a person who communicates by using these expressions. You will need to be aware of your own values as well as your own goals as you choose the most appropriate response.

Age and Affiliation

Because the continuity of life is valued in most cultures, respect for ancestors, the elderly, parents, and other significant others is frequently observed. The language used to render respect may vary from the use of private to formal forms. These forms may be directly related to practices in the home or in the external environment that recognize the dead or the living through prayer and certain expressions or greetings exchanged in the presence of the persons honored. Recognition of these forms in the language will tell you much about the beliefs and values of the culture of the people you are communicating with.

Most cultures, too, have a "set" of words and expressions best described as slang. Often these forms originate with a particular group and after some period of time reach the general society. These words may or may not be used by the majority of group members. They are, however, usually recognized and understood. Because these words usually emerge from a particular group, and often relate to particular events or activities, they may or may not be retained in the language. The popularity of these words usually decreases over time.

For the person who wishes to communicate effectively with others, it is important to be aware which slang phrases are appropriate, and which are inappropriate, and with which groups slang can be used, and with which groups slang cannot be used. Too, when a speaker uses slang in conversation with you, that slang may give you information about the speaker's background and experience that will help you to communicate more effectively.

SPEECH AND WRITING

References to the influence of speech on writing were made in Chapter 6. The relationship between linear and lateral preferences was emphasized and the importance of matching these approaches to the development of skills was introduced.

People who use linear approaches in their learning or work

setting may become adept at writing in a linear style. Because speech is linear, or the work or learning setting might require the use of linear skills, these skills may be seen to be highly developed in particular cultures and these skills may be reflected in their writing.

When people control the approaches to be used in developing their own writing skills, they often locate a method that works almost by accident, it may seem. If the direction is other-centered, or organized in the learning style of another person, the task may be more difficult, especially with persons who cannot make the shifts easily between left and right brain approaches. For this reason, tools like brain mapping or other lateral approaches may be helpful in teaching people to write or in learning to write using linear and lateral approaches. For our purposes it is helpful to know that the way people talk can be used to help them write; understanding the way they talk can also be useful to us in understanding their writing.

SKILL BUILDING

Close observance of speech patterns has been the focus of this chapter. Recognition of factors related to what people are telling us, how they are saying it, who is saying it, and under what circumstances, can help us identify our own learning needs.

Experience A: Observation Practice

Practice observing the relationship of language speech to intercultural communication by observing the patterns of other cultures within and outside of the United States. Select the areas of your choice from the list below.

1. Frequency and Duration of Language

2. Voice Quality and Sounds of Language

3. Informal and Formal Language

4. Special Group-Related Language

   Special Position-Related Language

5. One-to-One, and Small and Large Group Interaction

6. Racial-Ethnic Interaction

7. Gender-Related Interaction

8. Courtesy Language

What individual patterns were observed? Group patterns? How similar or different are your own patterns? The patterns of your culture? What do your observations reveal regarding your own ability to interact verbally with the people of the culture?

The importance of knowing the language of a particular area should not be underestimated. The language helps us understand the values of a people and these values will be reflected in their speech and events: their movies, songs, video and audiotapes; their drama, worship, and work.

Experience B: Discovering Values

During interaction with people from another culture, note the following.

1. **What** values are reflected?

2. **Where** (under what circumstances) were the values visible?

3. **How** were the values generally expressed or evidenced? Individually? By the group as a whole?

4. **Why** do you believe these values are important to members of the culture?

When attempting to discover values through observation of others, the identification and use of appropriate resources helps us meet present learning needs and uncover others. For our purposes, it is important to locate helpful people, places, or sites that offer resources such as literary and audiovisual materials, and seminars, courses, workshops, or other sources of related information.

Experience C: Matching Resources to Needs

Considering your observations in Experience A, and your responses to Experience B, complete the sentences below.

1. I need more opportunity to observe. . . .

2. My values are similar to those observed among the people of this culture because. . . .

3. My values are different from those observed among the people of this culture because. . . .

4. I need more information about the values of the people in this culture specifically related to. . . .

5. I believe the following resources would help me understand my observations and discoveries: (list specific resources in the chart below)

PEOPLE   PLACES   THINGS

SUMMARY

The balance of theory and practice presented in this chapter is, like that of the previous chapter, particularly suited to the language area of skill building. The observation practice in this chapter should also be helpful to you in the next. Chapter 7 was designed to help you move from knowledge to understanding and performance levels in your learning. How would you evaluate your progress? How will the commonality-diversity and individual-group relationships reviewed earlier apply to the development of your speaking skills?

CHAPTER 8

Gesturing

The focus of this chapter is on the recognition of nonverbal expressions of feeling or meaning in human interaction, and these expressions will all be categorized as "gestures." Considerations include cultural patterns with emphasis on facial and body positions and motions and the relationship of those observables to skill building.

Of the six skill areas present in this book, observation, speaking, and gesturing represent the areas that are most visible to others. We can value, listen, and think within ourselves but our eyes, speech, and body movements are recognized by others. These are the areas of ourselves open to others that illustrate our values and attitudes, that present a "picture" to others through our performance. Gestures speak without words.

NONVERBAL EXPRESSIONS AND GESTURES

Earlier we identified the nonverbal aspects of our living environments—the objects, sites, activities, and events present in our environments that reveal the values, not only of ourselves but of our culture. These nonverbal observables serve as resources for our skill development practice and represent the expressions of a people. In this chapter, we will look for the actions of people that speak without words so that the question of relationships will be complete and so that you will be able to identify additional components for your framework for action. The relationship of people to gestures is close and revealing and is an area worthy of our attention; this is an observable trait within our own and other cultures.

Although all people "speak without words," the language of the nonverbal is not the same as the verbal. That is, verbal language can be observed with defined, linear structures but nonverbal expression is more laterally oriented. Actions are personal and expressions and gestures are personal. The feelings that direct our expressions and gestures are, in turn, reflections of our values and are, as such, as individual as we are.

There are commonalities related to any study of gestures and expressions. We all have faces and bodies; we all register expressions and we all gesture. We know too that all people register happiness, sadness, or anger, or that they scowl or cry or smile. These expressions, however, may vary among the people of the world. How often have you misinterpreted an expression? Perhaps you have known people who appear sad, even when they are glad, or appear happy even when they are angry. Meanings based on our judgments can be ever so wrong where nonverbal observables are concerned. We are observing external expressions rather than feelings and our judgments are usually culture-specific. That is, we have reached our conclusions based on meanings commonly attached to particular expressions in our own cultures.

It is our meanings that differ. (That dual image again!) The language of nonverbal observables is as diverse as the cultures responsible for these meanings. For practical purposes, we should begin with a caution: Draw meanings from the **culture** regarding nonverbal expressions and gestures rather than from your cultural background or ours. There is a reason. Your expressions and gestures and ours are just as diverse as theirs. We only share common meanings within our own cultures. This means we'll have to discover the meanings through the people. It also means that, depending on our roles and degrees of interaction, we may not discover some of the meanings or expressions and gestures.

The Head and Face

The head and the face are an area of concern because speech is related to our faces and faces may reflect emotion—to greater or lesser degree—across all cultures and people. Eyes may be raised or lowered or move from one direction to another, meeting our eyes or turning away. Eyes close or open or widen or narrow and what does it mean? The meanings may vary and that's the fascinating part of the nonverbal observation game: from culture to culture the meanings of some movements are similar but the meanings of other movements are very different. In some cultures, the meeting of eyes is important. Parents or teachers may say "Look at me! Look at me!" and expect to be obeyed. In other cultures, children may be reprimanded for **not** looking down or away in the presence of some adults and others within the culture. Eye contact may be considered ill-mannered.

Eyes are but one part of the face that reflects meaning. Lip movements speak as loudly without words. Lips quiver, open, close, pucker, or move in more ways than we can count; they extend forward or backward or into a large smile. One of the best ways to observe lip movements is to observe a person speaking during a conversation. That might be an area of concentration for any of us because the words of various languages require a variety of lip movements, some quite common, but others more individualized or personal to their culture.

Facial movements involve the muscles and the muscles may be seen to involve the eyes and the lips. Faces can . . .

- glare
- frown
- grin
- cry
- stare
- flash a smile

Voices, too, come through the face and lips and are non-verbal observables. Voices can choke or tremble; voices can be . . .

- clear
- loud
- soft
- high pitched
- low pitched

Even the nose is involved in what happens to the face and to the voice. People sniff and voices may sound nasal.

The Body

The body uses space, and some reference has been made earlier to this use in discussion of movements that may occur during an individual's interaction with small or large groups. In all cultures the movements of the body are varied, demonstrating some commonalities but with variations to be observed in practice. People may walk quickly or slowly, with personal variations that involve swaying or upright, rigid positioning of the body. They may run but even then their movement may vary in terms of pace.

Placement of arms, hands, and fingers is another nonverbal observation area for your practice. Hands may be . . .

* touching
* trembling
* scratching
* drumming
* immobile
* making fists
* clasped

Legs and feet may be crossed. Legs may bend or become tense.

Robert Koch (1971, p. 289) listed 35 nonverbal behaviors in a study focused on teacher behaviors. This list may be helpful to you in determining what to observe:

1. Gestures
2. Hand movements
3. Foot movements
4. Voice variations
5. Silences
6. Facial expressions
7. Eye Language
8. Head movements

9. Nose movements
10. Lip movements
11. Postures
12. Gaits
13. Body shape and tone
14. Skin pallor, flushing, sweating
15. Tics
16. Territoriality shown
17. Proximity used
18. Handwriting
19. Art, drawing, doodling
20. Laughter
21. Breathing
22. Tactility
23. Prearranged signals
24. Clothes, hair, jewelry
25. Occupational stigmata
26. Use of time
27. Lack of essentials
28. Lack of expected reaction
29. Status moves or acknowledgment
30. Room appearance and arrangement
31. Modality for presenting lesson: visual, auditory, kinesthetic
32. Rituals and stereotyped behavior
33. Scratching, self-stroking
34. Toying with objects
35. Hesitations

Distance was among the nonverbal behaviors already high-lighted but should be considered here in terms of how close or how distant a person is in relation to the people in the environment. Who touches others? How often?

On the other hand, persons with sight impairments may develop other means of dealing with the environment. Touching becomes a habit in addition to other body movements that facilitate movement in the daily environment. Persons with other physical impairments often develop a "set" of nonverbal behaviors that enable them to function effectively.

CULTURAL PATTERNS

It should not be disconcerting to recognize the fact that nonverbal behaviors viewed across cultures should not be interpreted from the observer's viewpoint but from the viewpoint of how the expression or gesture is viewed within the culture. In describing the need for training in the development of observation skills related to nonverbal behavior, Dunning (1971, p. 256) referred to what he described as the "rules of the non-verbal game"; he suggested that "Understanding **what** is being conveyed can lead to understanding **why** it is conveyed."

Galloway (1971) noted the need to distinguish between words and the manner in which they are conveyed.

When a distinction is made between verbal information (words) and vocal nonverbal information (intonation, stress, length and frequency of pauses) it becomes apparent that the two modes of expression may not convey the same feeling within a single statement (p. 311). Sarcasm, for example, may contain a positive verbal message and a negative vocal message.

Nonverbal behavior has been described as a language of relationship. Similarities and differences in nonverbal behavior can be readily observed across cultures and observation in this area of relationships is a beginning; however, skill development must be ongoing if an understanding of the meaning of nonverbal behavior is to be achieved.

SKILL DEVELOPMENT

For practical purposes, your own development in this important area of human interaction need not be confined to observations of the people around you in the United States or within other cultures. Videotapes and films may be a valuable source of information and opportunities for practicing recognition skills. Audiotapes can be used to practice recognizing the relationship of sounds and language to nonverbal communication. The first step may be to identify your own needs in relation to the area of nonverbal communication, especially the recognition of nonverbal expressions and gestures and their varied meanings.

Establishing Meaning

Because the meaning of expressions and gestures is often culturally determined, interpretations must be based on understandings acquired both from the members of a particular culture and from external resources as well. The following practical, five-step approach may help persons outside a culture understand the commonly accepted expressions and gestures of the people within.

1. Assess your own learning needs.

2. Observe; compare and contrast similar situations.

3. Use appropriate resources.

4. Reach tentative conclusions.

5. Reevaluate your conclusions as necessary.

Building Skills

Although the areas of nonverbal observation may appear overwhelming at first glance, it is possible to determine the direction of your development by completing a brief needs assessment, the first step in the suggested approach.

Assessing Personal Needs

How would you describe your level of knowledge in the areas listed below? Assign ratings using the following: Low (L), Moderate (M), High (H).

1. My own gestures and expressions __; their meanings __

2. The accepted gestures and expressions of the people of my culture __; their meanings __

3. The accepted gestures and expressions of the people of the (a particular) culture __; their meanings __

Are you familiar with the accepted (local culture other than your own) expressions and gestures related to the human response areas listed below? Check Yes (Y) or No (N).

Happiness __   Embarrassment __   Anger __   Elation __
Regret __   Gratitude __   Contempt __ Politeness __
Mockery __   Friendliness __   Sadness __   Greetings __
Touching __   Kissing __   Yes! __   No! __
Please __   Thank-you __

Of the areas listed above, which related expressions and gestures are most important for you to know at this time? Which areas should be the focus of your learning at this time? Select one area and begin your development.

Observing: Comparing, Contrasting

The lists of observables described in this chapter will help you know what to look for in the environment around you or in the audiovisual resources you may have selected for practice. Daily life events provide a ready source of information. For example, events such as celebrations, birth or death experiences, study experiences, recreation or illness activities, work, or dining activities all offer observable opportunities for growth of communication skills.

Compare and contrast similar situations (for example, the celebration of birthdays in the United States and the celebration of birthdays in another national culture). How are the expressions and gestures similar? Different? Why?

Using Resources

Reference to resources enables you to expand your knowledge of the nonverbal expressions of a locality or to confirm or disclaim your observations and comparisons. People can—and, when willing, often will—offer a number of opinions. When seeking input, the idea is not so much to aim for "truth" but for variety of possible meanings for nonverbal behavior.

The use of carefully selected literary and audiovisual materials helps you pace your learning. The use of video or slide tapes and movies enables you to practice observation over extended periods of time. This approach is especially appropriate when interactive observation is not possible. In all situations, awareness of the values of a particular culture must be your primary concern and sensitive attention must be given to the meaning of local practices.

Reaching Conclusions

When you have completed your needs assessment and the information gathering stages of the process described above, you will be able to reach some tentative conclusions regarding your discoveries. The "rightness" or "wrongness" of your findings may not be so important at this stage as realizing what seems to make sense in terms of the information available to you. Premature or set conclusions interfere with the openness to discovery that is so important in intercultural communication. It is well to develop a predisposition toward discovery, particularly when improving your ability to recognize the nonverbal expressions and gestures of a people.

Reevaluating

You will need to reevaluate your learning experience (and maybe your learning needs) when

- you have difficulty discovering meanings because appropriate resources are not available;
- observation is restricted for whatever reasons; or
- your tentative conclusions have been up-turned!

Under certain conditions you may need to direct your learning toward (you guessed it) **patience.**

SUMMARY

The ability to recognize and to understand the meaning of nonverbal expressions and gestures within a culture may be a difficult skill to develop but it will be worth the effort. These observables enable you to **see** the people as they cannot be **heard**. But they must be heard for you to understand the full meaning of the behavior.

Part IV

The Third Phase of the Framework: Ongoing Learning

CHAPTER 9

Ensuring Future Growth

The framework for growth introduced in this book has been focused on you, your skills, and your future development as related to successful intercultural communication and interaction. An understanding of the relationship between commonality and diversity and of the individual to the group is necessary in the development of effective intercultural communication skills. Six skill areas were highlighted: valuing, observing, listening, thinking, speaking, and gesturing.

The challenge for any learner, however, rests in putting knowledge into action: that is, relating information to areas of personal need and practicing the necessary skills. The degree to which a learner is able to identify learning needs, to access related resources, and to match these resources to a preferred learning style is the degree to which individual learning goals will be achieved. For maximum benefit, this approach to learning should continue for a lifetime. Effective intercultural communication, however, is not only a learning but a teaching experience. The process is by nature an exchange or a sharing of meaning.

INTERCULTURAL COMMUNICATION: A LEARNING/TEACHING EXPERIENCE

The desire to apply knowledge has been frequently cited as a characteristic of adult learners and nowhere is this characteristic more evident than in intercultural settings. Whatever skills have been acquired are usually demonstrated. The success of the interaction depends on the skills present and the willingness of persons involved to discard ineffective habits and to acquire needed skills.

The process of discarding habits or "letting go" may be more difficult than acquiring new and necessary skills. Ineffective habits are not only frequently unrecognized but they have a tendency to "hang on" until replaced. For example, we tend to repeat practices learned during prior interaction until we receive negative verbal or nonverbal feedback. For this reason, interaction with individuals or groups of diverse cultural backgrounds is an ongoing learning experience, an opportunity for personal development, as well as an opportunity to share those skills necessary for balancing intercultural interaction. Interaction is both a teaching and a learning experience when we see ourselves as learners **first** and then as teachers when our own knowledge, skills, and attitudes are appropriately transferable; we are teachers when our knowledge, skills, and attitudes are related to the needs of others as perceived by others rather than by ourselves. We must decide if what we have to teach is what others want to learn and if what we have to share or to give is what others want to share or to receive.

We might not have difficulty in deciding how to proceed if people always . . .

- knew what they needed and wanted what they needed; or
- if people wanted what we think they need or want.

However, people often . . .

- want what they want and may or may not need,

and we often . . .

- don't know what they want or need, or
- don't know how to respond effectively to their identified wants or needs.

Successful intercultural interaction is a mutual learning and teaching experience. We learn as others teach and teach as others learn from our own value-based frameworks.

Within the United States of America

Our own learning can, and ideally should, begin in our own homes, organizations, and communities. Through recognition of our similarities and differences and individual and group relationships, we can begin to build needed skills and to effect successful relationships.

It is especially important to recognize the value of **travel** within the United States as a rich resource for skill building. Travel allows us to observe how the people of a pluralistic nation live, work, play, and learn. Travel enables us to listen to the speech of people of our multicultural population and from other cultures as well: they speak in our own assortment of languages, accents, and dialects from all parts of the country and often in languages from many other parts of the world.

Travel encourages us to appreciate the meaning of culture as we move from a larger to a smaller city or to a rural community, from poor to wealthy neighborhoods, or from businesses or factories to homes or places of worship. The culture of a people unfolds as we move along backroads and highways or on airplanes, buses, and trains.

After a 13,000 mile trip across the country in 1970, Bill Moyers (1971) described the urgent need for people within the United States to listen to each other. Writing later, Moyers captured the cultural values, moods, and complexities of the people he had encountered during his trip and emphasized their willingness to talk: "I found that most people not only hunger to talk, but also have a story to tell. They are not often heard, but they have something to say" (p. 341).

Often the people of our country "speak" through their businesses. These messages are particularly apparent in areas of the United States where demographic trends represent what Nathan Glazer, in an article by Kotkin (1987, p. 43), has called the "permanently unfinished story" of the United States of America. As the racial-ethnic composition of many cities rapidly changes, areas where the majority of residents were formerly of European descent may now have majority populations of Asian or Hispanic heritage.

Shifts in population may also be accompanied by shifts in

marketing approaches and practices. Kotkin (1987) noted the importance of recognizing cultural differences in bargaining, buying, or selling and in who makes the decisions in a particular group. "In the last analysis," Kotkin says, "that may be what marketing to minorities is really about."

> Be it the Mexican of El Monte or the Chinese of San Francisco or the Cubans of Little Havana, what 'minority' consumers respond to most eagerly is a level of respect that, too often, is missing in their transactions with mainstream businesses. Targeted advertising, bilingual salespeople, and special events all help to break down barriers. But their long-term value is to confirm for minorities that they are genuinely welcome and valued not just as consumers, but as people—and as Americans. (p. 47)

Whether listening to people on the road traveling or during interaction in ethnic neighborhoods, the use of the English language and the diversity of speech patterns and dialects is sure to offer a rich resource base for the interested learner. All sections of the United States provide variations that enable us to discover the values and attitudes of the people. These discoveries provide insight into a particular culture and may be keys to the customs and practices of the people. Alstad (1986) noted the tendency of settlers in the early American West to translate "The King's English into Cowboy Lingo with interesting results" (p. 14).

> Those earlier generations of Americans are now gone but their spirit lives on in the words they left behind. Colorful words that project the personality of the people who said them. Common sense words rooted in the old-time American principles of independent thinking. Slow-talking words, thoroughly chewed before using. Terse words from people with limited or no formal education, but words with a profundity and insight that today's best thinkers would be hard-pressed to meet or exceed. (p. 41)

Many of these expressions are readily understood and commonly used, even today, in particular areas. Often short—"You kin be wrong" (p. 18) or "Suspicion ain't proof" (p. 58)—these expressions may relate so directly to the culture that "outsiders" may find the language difficult to understand. For example, the expression "It's the little things that get tangled in your spurs that trip you up" (p. 136) might be unclear to anyone unfamiliar with such colloquial usage of the English language.

The relationship of language to settlements across the country may also be recognized in that of the Cajun French introduced by Acadian exiles from Nova Scotia in 1755 and spoken by these Americans of French, German, Spanish, and African-American heritage. Whatley and Jannise (1982) have noted the presence of German and Spanish surnames among today's Cajuns: names like "Huval, Schexnayder, Waguespack, and Zeringue" or Ortego, Diaz, and Romero. As the French language and culture was acquired by the people, so too the people influenced the expression of each in a variety of ways, such as in the development of the familiar Creole speech and in, for example, the introduction of the accordion into the music. A traditional German instrument, use of the accordion probably provided the most important German influence on Cajun music and it remains an integral part of today's Cajun bands (p. viii). Today, the "r" in Cajun French is a Spanish "r," reflecting the Spanish accent on the spoken French of the area (p. ix). Cajun words like "filé" (the spice commonly used in gumbo) and "bayou" reveal the Indian influence on Cajun French. African words like "gumbo" were also introduced and are part of the culture today.

Dealing with difference can be an exciting and valuable learning experience when personal skills enable us to discern values, to recognize needs or preferences, and to understand the roles people play within a particular culture or group. Dealing with difference can be an experience in learning to question and to seek answers. Who is involved here? Where? How? Why? What is valued here? Why?

The languages, customs, and beliefs of the original inhabitants of the United States of America are also a rich learning resource. North American Indian people in the United States represent many cultures, and individual and tribal values are reflected in the diverse practices and products of the people. An understanding of the influence of early, forced uprooting and resettlement on Indian and African-Americans can increase our understanding of the impact of similar uprootings abroad. An understanding of the relationship between individuals or groups and the land can be developed through a knowledge of recorded history and through focused conversations on the oral histories of the people. In a publication by the U.S. Government (1968), for example, attachment to the land was poignantly illustrated in the words of Barboncito, a Navajo Indian Chief, who during the council proceedings of the Navajo Treaty of 1868 lamented the tragic relocation of his people.

> I hope to God you will not ask me to go to any other country except my own. It might turn out another Bosque Redondo. They told us this was a good place when we came but it is not. (p. 5)

Whether sharing the experiences of people within the United States through reading or through conversation and interaction, the importance of recognizing the value of our diversity cannot be overestimated. People or the descendants of people are here who have survived hunger and degradation, poverty and enslavement, concentration camps and brutality. People or the descendants of people are here who understand the meaning of successful human interaction and communication because they know the meaning of inhumanity.

The systematic denial of sleep to Jews interned in a concentration camp, bringing them to a state of constant exhaustion, has been described by Pisar (1979). Noting the decimation of the camp's population and the tendency of persons to suddenly go raving mad from sheer lack of sleep, Pisar observed

> A human being faced with the harshness of nature will somehow manage to survive even against seemingly impossible odds. But when hardship is placed in his way by the deliberate act of his fellows, the solution to the problem often is beyond human reach. Even at its cruelest, nature is kinder than man touched by evil. (p. 87)

Dealing with difference can begin in the United States with the development of skills focused at knowledge and understanding levels and emphasizing the six primary skill areas. What really matters then is what we **do** with others to create effective interaction in the world we share.

Abroad

There are nonverbal observables that may account for a large number of our difficulties abroad as we interact with others. We hear ourselves speak and may make necessary adjustments but we can't see ourselves behave. We must rely on the reactions and responses of others in order to recognize the effect of our nonverbal behavior. The way we gesture, or approach the use of time, or respond to new foods may influence the responses of others.

In a description of difficulties encountered when doing business overseas, McCaffrey and Hafner (1985) cited the frustration of a group of account managers who were responsible for sales and marketing in an international travel business. They were concerned about the way their sales calls began in particular non-western countries. One person, especially, felt time was wasted with needless formalities and had tried to hurry the meetings along. McCaffrey and Hafner reported:

> It had not occurred to the account managers that the business people from the countries in question might actually consider these 'formalities' a critical part of business and not meaningless filler before the real work started. Nor did they consider that someone who tried to hurry through these formalities to get down to business might be considered rude, boorish and ultimately untrustworthy. (p. 27)

Such ethnocentrism may leave both sides feeling frustrated, and successful interaction as well as business transactions may be greatly diminished.

The recognition of similarities and differences related to **food** and eating practices is a personal and practical area of concern in ongoing skill development. Cross-cultural studies have shown that meals are designed according to particular cues based on odor, shape, color, temperature, or particular tastes and may have consistent structure within a given culture (Douglas, 1979). People, therefore, know what to expect. In some cultures, for example, the structure is spatial and foods may be arranged on the right, middle, and left of the dish. Other chronological structures of the meal may have a beginning, a middle, and an anticipated end. Our own eating patterns may or may not follow another culture's structure, thus causing difficulty for us when we miss the familiar cues.

Douglas (1979, p. 44) has observed "When we cross cultural barriers in dining, we may miss our accustomed stop signals and end up feeling either hungry or overstuffed." Douglas notes, too, that "Food taboos and preferences are rooted in the structure of our lives." Particular rules may be related to other rules concerning cleanliness, worship, or behavior in sex and marriage or social categories and occasions.

In some cultures, the distinction between hot and cold may be especially critical in any consideration of eating patterns. Cold items may or may not be served with hot items, for example, and serving utensils may or may not be heated to maintain a preferred temperature when serving a particular item of food or drink. Douglas (1979, p. 51) observed "the ceremonial and social purposes of meals may be more important than nutrition in determining diet."

Knowing the reasons for differences, however, does not necessarily equip the traveler with necessary coping skills. The business of coping may be especially difficult when attitudes and cultural practices must be maintained over extended periods of time. Knowing what might be served is not the same as being able to eat what is served or to enjoy it. For this reason, attentive practice has been suggested as an essential part of skill development. Early patterns and preferences were developed over a period of time and new patterns and preferences can be developed over a period of time. It is important, for example, to sample foods from a particular area **before** the actual visit, particularly if the cuisine is quite different from your own. It may even be important for you to try out recipes from a new area or culture if you intend to remain there for an extended period of time.

Cultures vary regarding their degrees of nonverbal expressiveness. For this reason attention should be given to how nonverbal observables are expressed and how often. Like eating practices, international gift giving customs fall into this category of observables. Knowing what to give, under what circumstances, and even whether or not to open a gift on receipt can be valuable knowledge during interaction abroad.

In the Parker Pen Company's *Do's and Taboos Around the World* (Axtell, 1985, p. 41), the importance of recognizing variations in response to body contact has also been noted and the observation that "touching can be a very touchy business" highlighted. Knowing when, where, and with whom to shake hands, for example, may be as important as knowing when, where, and whom to hug or to kiss. By increasing our knowledge of an area, its people, and our own learning needs, we can begin to practice the skills necessary for successful intercultural interaction. We know we're *ok*! It is in interaction with others that problems occur. So why not build a framework for effective action and give it a try by accessing appropriate resources?

FOCUSED SKILL DEVELOPMENT

The framework presented in this book not only is focused on learning and action but also is based on the assumption that learning is personal and, as such, is initiated and sustained by the learner. A second important assumption is that our relationship to our own culture must be recognized, even as we attempt to recognize the relationship of others to their respective cultures. Implicit is the realization that although we share many commonalities, we are, as individuals and often as groups, very diverse people as a whole.

Culture: Our Own and That of Others

Because our needs, values, preferences, and roles may be diverse, it is important in our own skill building to acknowledge the **parameters of personal judgments**. That is, we must recognize the limits of our ability to work alone in our development. We can benefit from the feedback others may offer. The importance of gathering the views of "insiders" in the development of cross-cultural orientation programs or in the completion of research has been described in a study by Brislin and Holwill (1977). The results of this study highlight the opinions of indigenous people regarding the writings (or opinions) of persons outside the culture and the importance of listening to the people of a particular culture to increase understanding.

Insiders in the study, for example, gave specific advice for better research and reporting of results; they suggested the need for researchers to learn the language and to talk to a wide variety of people; to be specific about the locations where data were gathered; to provide good evidence for generalizations and to avoid presenting situations that might be interpreted as typical of a given culture; to be careful when interpreting motives from behavior; and to read or to study the same materials that insiders read.

In another relevant study by Jeffres and Hur (1981), interpersonal communication was reported essential for maintaining ethnic communities and it was the major channel for the flow of information about an ethnic community. Exchanges between friends and neighbors and information from radio and daily papers, ethnic language papers or magazines, television programs, and churches were the primary means of providing news of an ethnic community. The people of a given culture and the media are important resources in skill development.

Recognition of gender roles in general and the roles of women in particular are an area of concern if we are to ensure personal growth and continued intercultural skill development. Although women in the United States have often been systematically excluded from international management assignments, women's roles have traditionally included the skills necessary for success overseas (Adler, 1979). Adler reported that although many male managers around the world may be unaccustomed to working with professional women, some cultures may have more extensive representation of women in the professional workforce than the United States. Some cultures may accord professional women from other countries particular status and, in others, the woman may assume primary economic and management responsibilities.

Although management in an international environment is different from managing domestically, Adler (1979) concluded the international manager needs access to a full range of behavioral and attitudinal skills traditionally linked to the male and the female roles within the culture of the United States. Female international managers are and can be effective overseas.

Just as it is important to recognize the management skills of women from the United States, it is important to recognize the role of women in many countries abroad as the primary producers of food. Because the very definition of women's appropriate economic role may be culturally determined or ambiguous, there is frequently no clear conception of the degree to which nonurban women are productive (Blumberg, 1979). The tendency to underestimate the economic contributions of the world's nonurban women may obscure the dimensions of women's roles in particular cultures as well. Present practices may be based on customs of the past that have not kept pace with change. In areas where change is slow, the contributions of women may be accorded lower status. For our purposes, it is well to discover what women and men actually do within the culture. An awareness of what has been recorded or documented is necessary as well as an awareness of missing information regarding the contributions of the people.

Culture: Past, Present, Future

The contributions of the past are visible in the present, and practices of the present may reflect the influence of the past. How do members of a particular culture render respect to ancestors or elders? How have practices of the past influenced the present? What is the relationship of these practices to practices in our own culture? Consideration of these and other questions will be helpful in determining areas of knowledge to be considered in the development of a framework for action or to ensure ongoing personal growth. How people behave today usually reflects the influence of the past and may hold implications for behavior in the future.

As the world becomes increasingly internationalized and people of many cultures become more aware of each other, the need to develop culturally sensitive skills becomes increasingly apparent. These skills can be developed and must be developed if we are to live, work, and learn together successfully. The key to learning, however, is engagement (Kidd, 1975): the close involvement of the learner with the task or subject matter, the human resource(s), and the environment.

LINKING RESOURCES TO LEARNING NEEDS

Skill development for each of us is related to our attitudes and preferences as well as to the ability to identify personal learning needs. The ability to identify, to effectively use, and to evaluate resources, however, is of key importance in satisfying our personal learning needs. This means looking for the people, places, and things that help us understand and appreciate a particular culture and then processing the related knowledge for understanding. It means using the understanding to develop appropriate behavioral responses.

Who can help us learn what we want to learn? What can help us best? Where will we find these valuable resources? The answers to these questions reside in the people and the environments that surround us but most of all in our readiness to search, to discover, and to match resources to needs wisely. Learning is personal.

In this book, the contributions of many people in fields related to our needs have been combined to create a framework for action, a framework focused on all of us, on our skills, and on our future development.

Cultural values are here to see,
Set in linear fashion;
Processed laterally.

REFERENCES

Adler, N.J. (1979). Women as androgynous managers: A conceptualization of the potential for American women in international management. *International Journal of Intercultural Relations, 3*(4), 407–472.

Alstad, K. (1986). *Savvy sayin's.* Tucson: Ken Alstad.

Axtell, R. E. (Ed.). (1985). *Do's and taboos around the world: A guide to international behavior.* Elmsford, New York: Benjamin.

Bateson, M. C. (1972). *Steps to an ecology of mind.* New York: Ballantine.

Blumberg, R. L. (1979). Rural women in development: Veil of invisibility, world of work. *International Journal of Intercultural Relations, 3*(4), 447–472.

Bochner, S. (1973). The house form as a cornerstone of culture. In R. W. Brislin (Ed.), *Topics in culture learning* (pp. 23–37). Honolulu: East-West Culture Learning Institute.

Brislin, R. W., & Holwill, F. (1977). Reactions of indigenous people to the writings of behavioral and social scientists. *International Journal of Intercultural Relations, 1*(2), 15–34.

Brookfield, S. (1983). *Adult learners, adult education and the community.* New York: Teachers College, Columbia.

Brown, I. C. (1963). *Understanding other cultures.* Englewood Cliffs: Prentice-Hall.

Buzan, T. (1974). *Use both sides of your brain.* New York: E. P. Dutton.

Chaze, W. L. (1980, October 13). Refugees stung by a backlash. *U.S. News and World Report, 89*(15), pp. 60–62.

Clinard, H. (1985). Listen for the difference. *Training and Development Journal, 39*(10), 39.

Coleman, J. S. (1977). Differences between experiential and classroom learning. In M. T. Keeton and Associates (Ed.), *Experiential learning: Rationale, characteristics, and assessment* (pp. 49–61). San Francisco: Jossey-Bass.

De Bono, E. (1983). The direct teaching of thinking as a skill. *Phi Delta Kappan, 64*(10), 703–708.

Douglas, M. (1979). Accounting for taste. *Psychology Today, 13*(2), 44–51.

Dunn, R., & Dunn, K. (1978). *Teaching students through their individual learning styles: A practical approach.* Reston, VA: Reston.

Dunning, G. B. (1971, October). Research in nonverbal communication. *The challenge of nonverbal awareness, 10*(4), 250–258.

Dyal, J. A., & Dyal, R. Y. (1981). Acculturation stress and coping: Some implications for research and education. *International Journal of Intercultural Relations, 5*(4), 301–327.

Edwards, B. (1979). *Drawing on the right side of the brain.* Los Angeles: J. P. Tarcher.

Edwards, B. (1986). *Drawing on the artist within.* New York: Simon & Schuster.

Feltz, W. (1975). Music for multicultural students. In R. W. Brislin (Ed.), *Topics in culture learning* (pp. 21–25). Honolulu: East-West Culture Learning Institute.

Fersch, S. (1974). *Learning about peoples and cultures.* Illinois: McDougal, Littel.

Galloway, C. M. (1971). The challenge of nonverbal research. *The Challenge of Nonverbal Awareness, 10*(4), 310–314.

Gardner, J. W. (1988). *Leadership: An overview.* Washington, D.C.: Independent Sector.

Gilligan, C. (1982). *In a different voice.* Cambridge: Harvard University Press.

Glaser, E. M. (1985, Winter). Critical thinking: Educating for responsible citizenship in a democracy. *National Forum, 65*(1), 24–27.

Goffman, E. (1974). *Frame analysis.* New York: Harper & Row.

Gregorc, A. F., & Ward, H. B. (1977, February). A new definition for individual: Implications for learning and teaching. *NASSP Bulletin,* pp. 20–26.

Hall, E. T. (1959). *The silent language.* Greenwich: Fawcett.

Hall, E. T. (1969). *The hidden dimension.* New York: Anchor Books.

Hall, E. T. (1976). *Beyond culture.* New York: Doubleday.

Hall, E. T. (1989). *The dance of life: The other dimension of time.* New York: Doubleday.

Jankovic, J., & Edwards, R. L. (1980). Understanding people through music. *Lifelong Learning: The Adult Years, 4*(3), 4–7, 31.

Jeffres, L. W., & Hur, K. K. (1981). Communication channels within ethnic groups. *International Journal of Intercultural Relations*, 5(2), 115–132.

Kasindorf, M. (1983, March 14). Hey haole, wassamattayou? *Newsweek, 101*(12), p. 49.

Kidd, J. R. (1975). *How adults learn*. New York: Association Press.

Knowles, M. S. (1970). *The modern practice of adult education*. New York: Association Press.

Knowles, M. S. (1975). *Self-directed learning: A guide for learners and teachers*. New York: Follett.

Knowles, M. S. (1980). *The modern practice of adult education: From pedagogy to andragogy*. Chicago: Cambridge.

Koch, R. (1971). Nonverbal observables. *The Challenge of Nonverbal Awareness, 10*(4), 288–294.

Kolb, D. (1976). *Learning style inventory*. Boston: McBer.

Kolb, D. (1983). *Experiential learning: Experience as the source of learning and development*. Englewood Cliffs, NJ: Prentice-Hall.

Korten, F. F. (1976). *Intercultural communication: A reader*. Belmont: Wadsworth.

Kotkin, J. (1987). Selling to the new America. *Inc., 9*(8), 43–47, 50, 52.

Kuralt, C. (1985). *On the road with Charles Kuralt*. New York: G. P. Putnam's Sons.

Leo, J. (1991, May 21). 'Diversity' tears oneness in two. *Rocky Mountain News*, p. 28.

Maslow, A. H. (1954). *Motivation and personality*. New York: Harper & Row.

McCaffrey, J. A., & Hafner, C. R. (1985). When two cultures collide: Doing business overseas. *Training and Development Journal, 39*(10), 26–31.

McCarthy, B. (1980). *The 4mat system: Teaching to learning styles with right/left mode techniques*. Oak Brook, Il: Excel.

Moyers, B. (1971). *Listening to America: A traveler rediscovers his country*. New York: Harper & Row.

Oberg, K. (1972). *Culture shock and the problem of adjustment to new cultural environments*. Pittsburgh: Regional Council for International Education.

Ornstein, R. E. (1972). *The psychology of consciousness*. New York: Viking.

Pisar, S. (1979). *Of blood and hope*. Boston: Little, Brown.

Renzulli, J. S., & Smith, L. H. (1978). Developing defensible programs for the gifted and talented. *Journal of Creative Behavior, 12*(1), 21–29 (ERIC Document Reproduction Service No. ED 110590).

Ricard, V. B. (1979). *ACCORD: A self-directed learning resource for the adult*. Unpublished doctoral dissertation, Union Institute, Cincinnati, Ohio.

Ricard, V. B. (1991). How effective intercultural communication skills can support learning. *Adult Learning, 2*(5), 13–14.

Samovar, L. A., & Porter, R. E. (1976). Communicating interculturally. *Intercultural communication: A reader*. Belmont: Wadsworth.

Samples, B. (1977). Mind cycles and learning. *Phi Delta Kappan, 58*(9), 688–692.

Singular, S. (1985, January 27). Stranger in a strange land: The Hmong experience in Colorado. *The Denver Post*, pp. 6–9, 12.

Sperry, R. W. (1968). Hemisphere disconnection and unity in conscious awareness. *American Psychologist, 23*(3), 723–733.

Stewart, E. C. (1975). *Aspects of American culture: Assumptions and values that affect cross-cultural effectiveness*. Pittsburgh: University of Pittsburgh, The Intercultural Communications Network.

Tannen, D. (1990). *You just don't understand*. New York: Ballantine Books.

Tannenbaum, R., & Schmidt, W. H. (1973). How to choose a leadership pattern—Retrospective commentary. *Harvard Business Review, 51*(3), 162–175, 178–180.

Tough, A. (1971). *The adult's learning projects*. Toronto, Ontario: The Ontario Institute for Studies in Education.

U.S. Government. (1968). *The Navajo treaty—1868*. Las Vegas: K. C. Publications in cooperation with the Navajo Tribe.

Walker, L. A. (1986). *A loss for words*. New York: Harper & Row.

Whatley, R. P., & Jannise, H. (1982). *Conversational Cajun French*. Gretna, LA: Pelican.

Wilson, M. (1983). *The effective management of volunteer programs*. Boulder: Johnson.

Witkin, H. A. (1974). *Field-dependence-independence and psychological differentiation: Supplement no 1*. New Jersey: Educational Testing Service (ERIC Document Reproduction Service No. ED 103459).

INDEX